REVISED and UPDATED
**NINTH EDITION**

# Getting into Films & Television

# Robert Angell

**how**to**books**

Published by How To Books Ltd,
Spring Hill House, Spring Hill Road,
Begbroke, Oxford OX5 1RX.
Tel: (01865) 375794. Fax: (01865) 379162.
info@howtobooks.co.uk
www.howtobooks.co.uk

Sixth edition (revised) 1999
Seventh edition 2002
Eighth edition 2004
Ninth edition 2009

British Library Cataloguing in Publication Data
A catalogue record for this book is available from the British Library

Cover photographs: grateful thanks to BAFTA, AMPAS, Mike Saunders, Campbell Mitchell, Daisy Gili and the London Film Academy. The British Academy award is based on a design by Mitzi Cunliffe
Produced for How To Books by Deer Park Productions, Tavistock
Typeset by PDQ Typesetting, Newcastle-under-Lyme, Staffordshire
Printed and bound by Bell & Bain Ltd, Glasgow

*Note*: The material contained in this book is set out in good faith for general guidance and no liability can be accepted for loss or expense incurred as a result of relying in particular circumstances on statements made in the book. The laws and regulations are complex and liable to change, and readers should check the current position with the relevant authorities before making personal arrangements.

# Contents

# List of Illustrations

# Foreword

The future of films and television depends to a very great extent on the talent, training and commitment of new entrants.

Robert Angell has, over the years, given advice to literally thousands of young people wanting to 'get into film or television'. In this most recent edition of his book he consolidates that advice based on his many years as a documentary producer who started in the cutting room and progressed through many different areas of production.

His book is as timely and welcome as when it first appeared, and I'm certain it will prove useful to future generations of professionals in an industry to which Bob and I have devoted our lives with almost manic obsession!

*David Puttnam*
(Lord Puttnam CBE)

# Preface
## to the Ninth Edition

When the first edition of this book was published, it was addressed primarily to people in the United Kingdom who were keen to take up a career in films and/or television in their own country.

In the intervening years, however, international production in all parts of the media has increased enormously and with the continuing growth of cable, satellite, multi-media and interactive forms of communication on discs or via the Internet, people should theoretically be able to train and work anywhere in the world. Some restrictions on complete freedom of movement do, of course, exist, imposed either by trade unions protecting the employment of their particular country's members or by immigration laws, work permits and so on which do not apply purely to film and television.

The actual business of making films and television programmes varies only marginally in different countries. Techniques may change slightly according to equipment used while names given to technical jobs and practices may not always be the same everywhere. For examples, 'Rushes' in the United Kingdom become 'Dailies' in the United States, while a 'Tracking Shot' becomes a 'Traveling Shot'.

But wherever you live and want to work, one thing is a common factor: getting your foot on the first rung of the ladder is equally difficult and competitive whether you have no training and elect to get in doing any job on offer and go for 'on the job' experience or have graduated from a film school or university in Britain, California, Warsaw or Manila. Whether you want to work in Europe, the United

States or Australia, the overall advice which forms the theme of this book is still valid.

There may have been technical advances and changes in some areas of production since the first edition of this book; its purpose is not to be a training manual, but to give the reader a flavour of different jobs in different aspects of production so that you can concentrate on trying to find a job in the area that interests you most.

This book, therefore, gives detailed descriptions of how films and television programmes are actually made in Britain, irrespective of the method by which they may finally be shown. It deals with feature films, commercials, documentaries, animation, multi-camera shooting and recording, OBs, events and news programmes with possible starting points in each area.

It also provides extensive information about training and practical advice about where and how to set about looking for a job.

Employment in film and television is open to everybody regardless of sex but some of the more physical jobs concerned with cameras, lights or building, for example, still attract very few women. Some of the job descriptions such as 'cameraman' are traditional but in Britain, the BBC, for example, has agreed that this term applies equally to men and women thus avoiding the cumbersome 'camerawoman' or worse still 'cameraperson'. If therefore in any part of this book, such titles as cameraman occur or there is any reference to 'he' as opposed to 'he' or 'she', there is absolutely no sexist insinuation intended and it should be stressed that all jobs are open to anyone regardless of sex, colour or background.

I am extremely grateful to a number of friends and colleagues in film and television for the help they have given me in writing this book, checking texts and providing material for illustrations.

Specifically, I would like to thank Paul Bradley, Siân Parry, Gillean Dickie and Freddie Korner of Merchant Ivory Productions; Ralph Sheldon; Ray Marshall, Michelle Durler and Linda Mattock of World Wide International; Marc Samuelson, Simon Shore, Jessica Parker and all at Samuelson Productions; Dan Zeff for features; Ash Wilkinson and Mark Leese, designers; John O'Driscoll of Paul Weiland Films; Mike Saunders, Geoff Edwards and Olly Wade for commercials; Bob Godfrey and Brian Stevens for animation; Alister Campbell and Jez Gibson of Visions for video post-production including *Harry*; Ray Galton, Alan Simpson and Douglas Argent for TV comedy; Steven Minchin for OBs and John Moulding of BBC News and Current Affairs for news programmes; Dave Dowler of Rank Laboratories for laboratory work; Roland Brinton of Partnership Films, and Ray Townsend of World Wide Pictures for documentaries; Alan Joy of Video Communications Consultants; Mike Bennett; IVCA; Oliver Dumas and Lucy Scott of Stage One Storyboards.

Finally, I would like to thank many schools and training organisations all over the world, particularly Stephen Bayly, Karin Farnsworth and Elizabeth Hardy of the NFTS; all at Skillset, Jobfit and FT2; and Fiona Russell, John Raymond, Roger Hammett, Polly Burlingham and their colleagues of BBC Training and Development.

*Robert Angell*

# Introduction

Films and television are two of the most powerful elements in the communications industry for they have the ability to entertain, inform and instruct in a very special way.

They may be addressed to an audience of one sitting at home in front of a television set or computer screen or an audience of many thousands in a darkened theatre seeing giant pictures engulfing them with the most powerful visual and sound images; and both extremes of audience numbers and every combination in between may be seeing anything from the most intense and lavish drama with a cast and crew of hundreds like *The Lord of the Rings* to a single talking head like an evening with the late Peter Ustinov, from the most dramatic news event like the first moon landing being seen as it actually happens to a complicated and carefully constructed teaching film on the most specialised subject like heart surgery for medical students.

- But there is one element common to all that makes these two media of film and television so unique – it is the **moving picture image.**

It is therefore essential for anyone wanting to become involved in the production of films or television in any capacity to realise that, in spite of the common factor of the moving picture, the various types of production are all separate and often some-what self-contained cottage-style industries.

So the first thing for any prospective newcomer to decide is what particular aspect and what type of production interests you most. To help you in this, you might try what might be called 'the magic wand trick'.

Imagine that all your ambitions could be realised and by means of a magic wand you are propelled forward in time, say ten years. What would you like to be doing most of all?

Directing epics like *James Bond* movies, photographing wild life documentaries, writing scripts for training films for BP or designing sets for classic costume dramas?

By this means, the planning of your career path can be better defined and you may possibly avoid some wasted time, energy and money seeking employment in production areas far removed from your ultimate ambition.

That is not to say that cross-fertilisation is not possible within both film and television and many a director has moved from documentary to drama, many an editor from post-production to directing. But, sadly, there is still quite a gulf between, for example, the world of live TV production and the more meticulous and slower type of work on film making in a studio. There are, of course, many elements common to all types of production and with improvements in High Definition, video and DVD (digital video disc) technology and changes in fashion and style, the possibilities for moving from one sort of production to another are increasing all the time.

But very often it is the area where you start which may influence very strongly the course your career may subsequently take. So whether you think you know exactly where your ambitions lie or whether, like many, you just know you want to be involved in some way in the business of film and television, the aim of this book is to give you a taste of the various jobs in different types of production and then suggest routes that you might take to get a foothold in your chosen area.

# 2

# Feature Films

## PRE-PRODUCTION – THE FOUNDATIONS

### What is a feature film?

A feature film is one with running time of not less than 90 minutes made usually on 35mm film and intended primarily for release in cinemas. Subsequent release on all types of television – satellite and cable – and release on video or DVD now form such an increasing part of any long term distribution of a feature film that it may also be a substantial part of the financial package.

### The treatment

So how does a feature film come about? The script may be based on an existing work – a book or play – or may be an original, but whatever the source, the initial document on which interest is roused is called a **treatment** (see sample on page 9). The best way to describe a treatment is to imagine that you are viewing a feature film and then have to write a precis in prose describing in the most visual terms possible the plot and characters. The difference for the scriptwriter is that he only has his imagination to call on at this stage.

The treatment may be enhanced with more detailed descriptions of the characters and their relationships in an introduction

4

and some initial presentations may go further than a treatment, be in two columns and termed an outline script. The two columns which are common practice (or ought to be!) in all forms of script usually show the action or picture on the left and the sound (dialogue, music and/or sound effects) on the right.

## THE SCRIPTWRITER

We now come to the basic problems facing the untried or budding scriptwriter.

1.  How far should you go at this stage speculatively?

2.  What is the most suitable presentation?

3.  To whom should you send your idea?

The recommendations are as follows.

### Script development stages

The normal development stages for a script are:

(a) Treatment

(b) Outline script

(c) Dialogue script

(d) Shooting script

The scriptwriter eventually has to be prepared to go as far as (c) and (d) above, but (d) may be written by the director who is ultimately responsible for the overall creative content of the film and may want to work out in detail (perhaps in collaboration with the writer) the precise planning and timing of each shot.

The first question usually asked when seeing a film or television programme being made is, 'What on earth do all these people do?' The chapters that follow in this book help to demystify all the creative, technical and craft jobs in these industries, concentrating particularly on possible starting points for anyone wanting to make it in Films or Television.

The silhouette illustration is reproduced with the kind permission and assistance of Neil Roe and the Museum of the Moving Image, London.

So how far should you go speculatively? The answer should probably be only as far as (a) and (b) although you may be tempted by anyone showing signs of interest who finds it easy to say 'I'd like to see the idea developed more fully'. It can however be argued that a treatment or outline script ought to be sufficient to judge the potential and enough for the producer to raise **seed money** for the project. Seed money is finance to enable a dialogue and shooting script to be commissioned, for a director to do some initial work and for more detailed location surveys to be carried out and a budget to be worked out. But seed money has always been extremely difficult to find because there is still the greatest risk and very few of the pieces of the jigsaw may be in place.

## Pieces of the jigsaw

Here are some of the disparate pieces which may be a long way from fitting together.

- Who is the most suitable and bankable director and will he be available at the time when the production might be scheduled?

- Who are the most suitable and bankable actors and will they be available?

- Will the right director and actors come together in order to attract and satisfy finance for the production?

- Where will the finance be found and on what terms?

## What is the most suitable presentation?

The most suitable presentation for which a scriptwriter should

**Thirty Things to Do Before You're 30**

*...Spend a night in a police cell*
*Stop taking your washing home to your Mum*
*Give up wearing leather trousers*
*Fire a gun*
*Write off a car*
*Have sex with someone famous*
*Visit at least three continents*
*Have sex on at least three continents...*

**LEAH** is a journalist who writes for a lads' magazine. She's used to compiling these lists; it's a laugh, it's what her readers like.

She met her boyfriend Cass four years ago and has since become the centre of attention with his mates; enjoying the banter in the pub when the soccer team meet on Sundays (and at the same time keeping in touch with her readers...). She's always been her own person – dynamic, independent and confident – but now she's pregnant and her perspective is changing. She's realised that she needs to know what men *really* think about life...and one man in particular.

**CASS** loves her to bits and they're great together, but this pregnancy thing is a bit scary for him. The eternal lad, he's finding it hard to come to terms with the impending responsibility, especially as it has happened just as his business is finally taking off. His solution is to flirt with every woman he meets (even hitting on Leah's midwife), eventually managing to have a one night stand with a beach volleyball player he meets on a weekend away with the soccer team. None of this helps his relationship with Leah, of course, and it also forever changes things with his best and oldest friend, Adam.

**ADAM** is also Leah's ex, so there has always been unresolved tension between him and Cass. When Cass starts misbehaving, Adam sides with Leah and the lads' friendship is stretched to the limit. However, there is more at stake than that; Adam has finally decided to tell his mates that he is gay. A lot of people already know, and he's quite cool and happy about it; it's just that he's never told his Sunday soccer mates. How can he tell them he's queer? After all, they've been playing together since they were 9 – an incredible 20 years. Twenty years of lying to his mates. If the team breaks up, which seems likely as they approach their 500th game, will he never get the chance to tell them? And then – the crunch – will he have the nerve to tell Cass that he is in love with him?

**DYLAN** thinks he's used his 29 years wisely – he's a classically trained musician for God's sake. Shame he can only get a weekly jazz gig in a pub; especially when his father, **MONTGOMERY**, is such a fantastically successful businessman and a very cool guy, who always puts Dylan in the

**Fig. 1. Pages from a treatment.**

shade. Dylan's self-confidence builds, though, when he meets the woman of his dreams — the beautiful, independent minded, intelligent **CLAIRE** — only to be shattered when he discovers that she's about to marry his father. The quiet and serious 'intellectual' of the team, he makes an odd couple with his flatmate Colin.

**COLIN,** good-looking but a bit thick, didn't realise he had a problem about his twenties coming to an end. But, helping Leah with her list of 'things to do' makes him realise that he is a bit boring and, for the first time in his life, gives him an ambition: to have a threesome before he is 30. When his girlfriend, the sexy and vivacious **VICKY,** introduces him to **SHEERA** he thinks he's in with a chance, but things don't quite work out according to his plans.

**BILLY**'s different from the rest of the lads in the team. At 29 he's the only one who's married — and he has two great kids. Some of the lads think he's got it all, but that's not how he sees it. His marriage to his childhood sweetheart **KATE** comes under strain because he seems to be more interested in Sunday football than in renovating their dream home. But when, in sad circumstances, she eventually witnesses the close friendship between the lads, Kate realises that it is much more than football which has kept them together.

**JOHNNY**'s also about to turn 30. He's fit, athletic, robust, just like his father **DON** used to be. But now Don's dying, and Johnny can't handle it. So much so that he won't take him to watch the lads play football, even though it was Don who started the team all those years ago. It's only when **FIONA** (Don's home carer, whose presence Johnny has resented) tells him that the team is all Don has to live for that Johnny realises how much he loves his Dad. Don is the emotional force behind the team and all the boys feel a fierce loyalty to him; at his funeral Johnny accepts just how much they all owe to his Dad.

The thrust of the story follows the lads' numerous attempts to play the team's 500th match. But this is not a film about football (in fact we never see a ball being kicked!). It's a warm-hearted, funny, romantic story about friendship and love, loss and redemption. Played out against the backdrop of London — not the grimy, depressing world of many such tales, but the vibrant, exciting, cosmopolitan place it can also be — it's about ordinary people trying to make sense of their messy lives.

Things to do before you're 30: Realise this isn't a dress rehearsal — GET A LIFE!

**Fig. 1. Pages from a treatment (continued).**

Johnny can't help grudgingly smiling - he's glad to see the old man.

> PARAMEDIC
> Do you need a hand to get him
> into -

> JOHNNY
> (curt)
> We're fine, thanks.

The other paramedic hands Johnny a small suitcase and they go back to the ambulance.

> DON
> Did you win this morning?

A beat.  Johnny contemplates his father looking frail in the wheelchair.  He makes a decision... to lie.

> JOHNNY
> Didn't play.  In fact, I've
> jacked it in.  We all have.

> DON
> 'Course you have.

But Johnny's not smiling.

> DON (cont'd)
> Is this for real?  I... go into
> hospital for a couple of months
> and...

And Johnny wheels Don briskly towards their flat as the ambulance pulls away.

> DON (cont'd)
> Cass has quit?  Adam?

> JOHNNY
> They've all packed it in.


10   EXT/INT. FRONT OF BILLY'S HOUSE/BILLY'S CAR - DAY                                 10

Billy is now asleep in the car as the soccer commentary drones on.  Through the windscreen, we see a woman in her late twenties coming out of the front door of the cottage.  Dressed in paint spattered overalls - her hair a mess, tied up in a scarf - this is DEBORAH, Billy's wife.  She spots Billy.

(CONTINUED)

**Fig. 2. A page from a dialogue script.**

establish interest is a treatment. This is advisable for two reasons:

### Providing sufficient information

It ought to provide sufficient information on plot, characters and style to allow assessment by a director or producer. Equally, it should not be so long that it provokes the easy excuse 'I haven't had time to read it' from established film people who are normally very busy and may have a pile of scripts submitted from all over the world.

### Copyright

It is very difficult to establish proof of copyright on a treatment but the front page should state clearly the title and underneath, 'A treatment for a feature film', the author's name and address and the word 'copyright' or the acknowledged symbol © and the date.

Proof of copyright can also be established as follows:

- Posting yourself a copy by registered post.

- Lodging a copy with the Union, BECTU, 373–377 Clapham Road, London SW9 9ET. Tel: (020) 7346 0900.

- Seeking advice from the Writers' Guild of Great Britain. Their address is: The Writers' Guild of Great Britain, 15 Britannia Street, London WC1X 9JN. Tel: (020) 7833 0777. Website: *www.writersguild.org.uk*

## To whom should I send my idea?

Log on to *www.thescriptvault.com* and seek advice from *The Scriptwriter* magazine (see Appendix).

## *Directors*

Study the work of film directors and also read the trade papers (see Appendix) to see whether directors you think might be interested are just starting or in the middle of a production. Every director thinks about his next project but the more prestigious the director, the more choosy he can be. Nevertheless, good ideas and good writing are still at a premium.

Directors do not like to be 'type cast' but obviously they may develop some continuity of style and therefore it may be foolish to send an idea for a very small scale parochial drama to a director renowned for big budget science fiction epics. Equally, your idea might be a mould breaking one that appeals.

How do you contact directors? In Britain via:

The Directors' Guild of Great Britain, 4 Windmill Street, London W1T 2HZ. Tel: (020) 7580 9131.
Email: *guild@dggb.org*

The Broadcasting Entertainment Cinematograph and Theatre Union (BECTU), 373–377 Clapham Road, London SW9 9BT. Tel: (020) 7346 0900.

The British Academy of Film and Television Arts (BAFTA), 195 Piccadilly, London W1J 9LN. Tel: (020) 7734 0022.

New Producers Alliance, 7.03 Tea Building, 56 Shoreditch High Street, London E1 6JJ. Tel: (020) 7613 0440.
Email: *queries@npa.org.uk*

If a director is interested in your script, he will know the producer or production company with whom he prefers to work and will introduce you.

## *Producers*

You may however choose to make a direct approach yourself and send your idea to a producer, especially if you do not know a suitable director.

This is perhaps the moment to clarify the exact role of a producer on a feature film.

The producer is in overall charge of the project, selecting and employing the key creative people – the writer, director, cameraman, art director and principal actors and actresses, all of these in collaboration with the director who may himself have been selected by the producer or may come to the producer with the project.

The producer is responsible for raising the finance and subsequently supervising the expenditure, keeping backers and investors happy with how their money is being spent. He is also concerned with keeping a happy atmosphere in the unit as a whole, keeping the project within schedule and budget, taking responsibility if an extension of either is justified.

He is not directly concerned with creative and artistic aspects of the film but his judgement in these matters, especially when it is mixed with financial considerations, should be appreciated and accepted by those in creative positions.

Extremely amicable relationships develop between producers and directors, where each respects the extent of the other's responsibilities, for both, and indeed the whole unit, should have exactly the same ultimate aim – to produce the finest film which will appeal to the widest audience in spite of often irksome restrictions in budget and schedule.

By sending your script to a producer, if the idea appeals, he will be responsible for providing the seed money and he will then be the person who will draw up a contract for you either by acquiring your treatment or commissioning you to develop it further.

Try to find those companies that concentrate on the production of feature films. This is sometimes difficult as directories do not always break down companies into categories and some further research may be necessary.

## THE FILM STARTS TO COME TOGETHER

Following the progress of an imaginary feature film, let us assume that a producer who owns or works for a production company has a director who is interested in a subject and seed money has been obtained to acquire rights from a writer, a script developed and a budget prepared.

We now come to what has all too often proved to be the most difficult and sometimes the most lengthy part of feature film production – the raising of production finance and negotiating the deals attached.

In the great days of Hollywood, the majors operating from their own studios provided the package which followed a well-tried formula of a good script, a well-known director plus some of their contract stars who would virtually guarantee the loyalty of an audience. Thus the business side of finding the finance was more straightforward, only hampered by the whims of the moguls and their stars who could dictate completely the creative content of the film and even cancel a complete production at any stage.

In Britain, the same situation prevailed to a lesser extent through dealings with the major distributors of films, both US and British, some of whom also owned studios. A percentage of finance obtained from a **distributor**, who is the equivalent of a wholesaler in industry, guaranteed a release of a film to one of the major circuits often because they also owned the cinemas.

The owners and operators of cinemas are called **exhibitors** but as these became fewer and more fragmented, finance or a guarantee from a distributor no longer ensured that the film would receive a wide showing, thus making the whole proposition less attractive to investors who were prepared to top up the whole package.

Most countries, in order to encourage a native film industry whose products may be great potential exports as well as sometimes being good public relations, provide tax incentives for investors; in Britain arrangements have only fairly recently come into force to encourage investment.

So how does a producer find the finance? Increasingly, the BBC and other television organisations have followed the brave initiative of Channel Four and financed feature films in whole or in part either through their own subsidiaries or through independent companies. The attraction, apart from the profits possible through world wide cinema release, is the option on the television and ancillary rights which now form an increasing part of the total package.

Apart from these sources, merchant banks, the pre-sale of some TV or other rights and even private investors may be involved. If the subject invites co-production, this has become increasingly popular with multifarious interests from anywhere in the world.

# STATEMENT OF PRODUCTION COST

Production Company ................................................ Period............ ended..............................

Title of Film......................................................

| | COST HEADING | Cost this period | Accrued Cost to date | Estimate to Complete | Estimated Final cost | BUDGET | Over/under Budget |
|---|---|---|---|---|---|---|---|
| 1 | "ABOVE THE LINE" COSTS: | | | | | | |
| A | STORY AND SCRIPT | | | | | | |
| B | PRODUCER FEES | | | | | | |
| | DIRECTOR FEES | | | | | | |
| E | PRINCIPAL ARTISTES | | | | | | |
| | Sub-total | | | | | | |
| 2 | "BELOW THE LINE" COST: | | | | | | |
| C | PRODUCTION UNIT SALARIES: | | | | | | |
| | 1. Production Management & secretaries | | | | | | |
| | 2. Asst. Directors and Continuity | | | | | | |
| | 3. Technical Advisers (incl. Choreographers) | | | | | | |
| | 4. Camera Crews | | | | | | |
| | 5. Sound Crews | | | | | | |
| | 6. Editing Staff | | | | | | |
| | 7. Stills Camera Staff | | | | | | |
| | 8. Wardrobe Staff | | | | | | |
| | 9. Make-up Artist | | | | | | |
| | 10. Hairdressers | | | | | | |
| | 11. Casting | | | | | | |
| | 12. Production Accountancy | | | | | | |
| | 13. Projectionists | | | | | | |
| | 14. Miscellaneous Studio Staff | | | | | | |
| | 15. Foreign Unit Technicians | | | | | | |
| D | ART DEPARTMENT SALARIES | | | | | | |
| E | ARTISTES: | | | | | | |
| | 1. Cast (Other than Principals) | | | | | | |
| | 2. Stand-ins, Doubles, Stuntmen | | | | | | |
| | 3. Crowd | | | | | | |
| F | MUSICAL DIRECTION, MUSICIANS, ETC. | | | | | | |
| G | COSTUMES AND WIGS | | | | | | |
| H | MISC. PRODUCTION STORES (EXCL. SETS) | | | | | | |
| I | FILM STOCK & LABORATORY CHARGES | | | | | | |
| J | STUDIO RENTALS | | | | | | |
| K | EQUIPMENT | | | | | | |
| L | POWER | | | | | | |
| M | TRAVEL AND TRANSPORT: | | | | | | |
| | 1. Location | | | | | | |
| | 2. Studio | | | | | | |
| N | HOTEL AND LIVING EXPENSES: | | | | | | |
| | 1. Location | | | | | | |
| | 2. Studio | | | | | | |
| O | INSURANCES | | | | | | |
| P | SOCIAL SECURITY ETC. | | | | | | |
| Q | PUBLICITY SALARIES AND EXPENSES | | | | | | |
| R | MISCELLANEOUS EXPENSES | | | | | | |
| S | SETS AND MODELS: | | | | | | |
| | 1. Labour – Construction | | | | | | |
| | 1a. Materials – Construction | | | | | | |
| | 2. Labour – Dressing | | | | | | |
| | 3. Labour – Operating | | | | | | |
| | 4. Labour – Striking | | | | | | |
| | 5/6. Labour – Lighting and Lamp Spotting | | | | | | |
| | 7. Labour – Foreign Unit | | | | | | |
| | 8. Properties | | | | | | |
| T | SPECIAL EFFECTS | | | | | | |
| U | SPECIAL LOCATION FACILITIES | | | | | | |
| | | | | | | | |
| | Sub-total | | | | | | |
| 3 | INDIRECT COSTS: | | | | | | |
| Y | FINANCE AND LEGAL FEES | | | | | | |
| Z | OVERHEADS | | | | | | |
| | TOTAL | | | | | | |

Signed .................................................... Date ...........................

## Fig. 3. Feature budget form (excerpt).

## Branagh's 'Henry V'

One of the most novel projects as far as finance was concerned was Kenneth Branagh's *Henry V*. Calling on its experience as a kind of up-market repertory theatre, Renaissance Film Productions, the off-shoot of the theatre company of the same name, set about raising finance in comparatively small amounts from individuals, rather like the system of 'angels' in the theatre. The success of the film leads one to hope that more feature films could be set up in this way, thus avoiding some of the crippling interest charges on loans that often accompany other forms of finance which, in turn, delay interminably the arrival of the break-even figure before all those involved in the project begin to see any profit.

There is another factor peculiar to the film industry: the producers of the film, who are the equivalent of manufacturers in industry, are the last in the chain to receive any money. The exhibitors take the money at the box office and this is termed the gross. The distributors who have made the arrangements with the cinemas then take their percentage, leaving the balance (the net) to go to the producer who is first faced with

- recovering the production cost of the film and

- paying off interest charges which may have formed part of the package.

It is not suggested that any newcomer will necessarily be involved in this wearisome business of raising finance but it will give you some idea of the possible time involved from the moment that somebody has a good idea to when the cameras actually start to roll.

It will also give you an indication of how far down the line individuals can be whose contract gives them a share of the producer's net profit. For only after all the costs mentioned above have been met, can the producer's share of the profit be termed 'net'.

## THE PRODUCTION STARTS

So let us assume that the finance is in place or, as often happens, enough is there with the balance waiting to be formally agreed but sufficiently certain for the production to move forward to the next stage of preparation.

### The production company

If the film is largely to be shot in the studio, or even only partly, the production company, as part of a deal to hire the studio, will in all probability have production offices included and possibly an editing suite for the editing as well. Sometimes companies are specially formed for the production of just one feature film. This is convenient for accounting and separating all the deals which have been made over the finance but makes it harder for the newcomer contacting companies when you may discover that a company is only operating in a semi-dormant state after the film has been completed.

#### Production staff

The production company, then, is installed in its production offices, a production manager and a production secretary (may be called a production supervisor or production co-ordinator) engaged. The job of production manager is the most responsible administrative and organisational one on a feature film under the producer and, if the film is very complex, there may be associate producers to help with this side of things. The production manager will probably have already worked with the producer on the budget (see Figure 3 page 17) and a production accountant and so his next task is to prepare a breakdown of the script and a shooting schedule (see Figure 4 page 21) bearing in mind continually the constraints of the budget on the latter.

## Breakdown

The breakdown consists broadly of studio shooting, subdivided further into the various sets and artists involved, location interiors and exteriors also with or without artists, whether shots are with sound recording (synch) or silent (mute), an estimate of the time allowed in hours or days and finally, any special requirements in the way of equipment (camera cranes, helicopters and mounts for example) or personnel (stunt men, special effects and so on).

## Design

The production secretary works closely with the production manager obtaining information on his behalf like prices, permissions, hotels, insurance and transport and coping with the mounting crescendo of correspondence and copying.

Here additional staff may join the team as secretaries for, in parallel with this, the designer will have been appointed and be starting work with the director on sets for the studio or re-vamping location interiors and exteriors.

On location surveys, the director and designer will probably be accompanied by the production manager and possibly the first

| | | | | | | |
|---|---|---|---|---|---|---|
| | **--- END OF DAY 20 -- Thu, Oct 2, 2003 -- 4 6/8 pgs.** |||||| 

**--- END OF DAY 20 -- Thu, Oct 2, 2003 -- 4 6/8 pgs.**

**SPLIT DAY 10.00 HRS - 21.00 HRS**

| Scene | | Description | | Time | Pages | Cast |
|---|---|---|---|---|---|---|
| 60 | IOM | EXT LAYBY - JOHNNY'S CAR<br>JOHNNY GETS THE CAR STARTED. | | Day | 3/8 pgs. | 6, 12 |
| 60A | IOM | EXT ROAD NR F YARD FC - JOHNNY'S CAR<br>JOHNNY PULLS AWAY - DON @£$%^ | | Day | 1/8 pgs. | 6, 12 |
| 27 | IOM | I/E SQUAT - ENTRANCE / HALLWAY / LOUNGE<br>COLIN CAN'T BELIEVE THE STATE OF THE PLACE | | Night | 6/8 pgs. | 5, 8, 17 |

**--- END OF DAY 21 -- Fri, Oct 3, 2003 -- 1 2/8 pgs.**

**END OF WEEK 4**

**SHOOT MAIN CROWD SHOTS THIS DAY**

| Scene | | Description | | Time | Pages | Cast |
|---|---|---|---|---|---|---|
| 73 | IOM | EXT STADIUM - PITCH - 500TH GAME<br>PRE MATCH PIECE TO CAMERA | | Day | 2/8 pgs. | 32 |
| 73E | IOM | EXT STADIUM - PITCH - 500TH GAME<br>FLIRTY TV PRESENTER REJECTED - CASS ADAM TO BE GOD F/ | | Day | 2 pgs. | 1, 3, 4, 32, 33 |
| 73B | IOM | EXT STADIUM - 500TH GAME<br>DYLAN AND COLIN ENJOY ATMOSPHERE - MONTGOMERY AND | | Day | 2/8 pgs. | 2, 8, 14, 15 |
| 73D | IOM | EXT STADIUM - 500TH GAME<br>MONTGOMERY AND DYLAN 'MAN TO MAN' - DYLAN CONGRATI | | Day | 2 pgs. | 1, 2, 6, 14, 15, 32 |

**--- END OF DAY 22 -- Sun, Oct 5, 2003 -- 4 4/8 pgs.**

**P/U SCENES 73 ETC NO CROWD**

| Scene | | Description | | Time | Pages | Cast |
|---|---|---|---|---|---|---|
| 73A | IOM | EXT STADIUM - 500TH GAME - CAR PARK<br>BOYS GATHER FOR THE GAME - FIONA ARRIVES | | Day | 2/8 pgs. | 4, 6, 13 |
| 73C | IOM | EXT STADIUM - 500TH GAME - CAR PARK<br>JOHNNY'S CHUFFED FIONA'S THERE | | Day | 4/8 pgs. | 3, 4, 6, 7, 13, 18, 36 |

**--- END OF DAY 23 -- Mon, Oct 6, 2003 -- 6/8 pgs.**

| Scene | | Description | | Time | Pages | Cast |
|---|---|---|---|---|---|---|
| 75 | IOM | INT STADIUM - TUNNEL 500TH GAME<br>THEY COULD JUST PLAY ONCE A YEAR AS A MEMORIAL | | Day | 2 pgs. | 1, 2, 4, 5, 6, 7, 8, 9, 10, 16, 36 |
| 74 | IOM | INT STADIUM - CHANGING ROOM (3) 500TH GAME<br>AT LAST-THE BOYS PREPARE FOR THE 500th GAME | | Day | 2 pgs. | 1, 2, 4, 5, 6, 7, 8, 9, 10, 16, 18 |

**--- END OF DAY 24 -- Tue, Oct 7, 2003 -- 4 pgs.**

**SPLIT DAY 13.00 HRS - 24.00 HRS**

| Scene | | Description | | Time | Pages | Cast |
|---|---|---|---|---|---|---|
| 35 | IOM | EXT COUNTRY HOTEL/CAR PARK<br>RAINING - THE BOYS RUN INTO THE HOTEL. | | Day | 2/8 pgs. | 1, 2, 4, 6, 7, 8 |
| 36 | IOM | INT COUNTRY HOTEL/ RECEPTION<br>THE HOTEL BEGINS TO APPEAL WHEN THEY SEE A GIRL CROSS | | Day | 1 4/8 pgs. | 1, 2, 4, 6, 7, 8, 27 |
| 37 | IOM | INT COUNTRY HOTEL/BAR<br>COLIN KNOWS THE GIRLS - THINGS ARE LOOKING UP. | | Day | 4/8 pgs. | 1, 2, 4, 6, 7, 8, 25, 26, 27 |
| 38 | IOM | INT COUNTRY HOTEL/BAR<br>EVERYONE IS GETTING ON WELL | | Night | 2 4/8 pgs. | 1, 2, 4, 6, 7, 8, 25, 26, 27 |

**--- END OF DAY 25 -- Wed, Oct 8, 2003 -- 5 6/8 pgs.**

**NIGHT SHOOT - 18.00 HRS - 05.00 HRS**

| Scene | | Description | | Time | Pages | Cast |
|---|---|---|---|---|---|---|
| 39 | IOM | EXT COUNTRY HOTEL/GARDEN/TERRACE<br>SURREAL FOOTBALL MATCH - ADAM TELLS KYLIE HE IS GAY | | Night | 1 7/8 pgs. | 2, 4, 6, 7, 8, 26, 27 |
| 41 | IOM | EXT COUNTRY HOTEL/GARDEN/TERRACE<br>THE OTHERS HEAR A GIRL YELLING | | Night | 4/8 pgs. | 2, 4, 6, 7, 8, 26, 27 |
| 40 | IOM | I/E COUNTRY HOTEL/CAR PARK/PEOPLE CARRIER<br>CASS & TINA AT 'IT' | | Night | 4/8 pgs. | 1, 25 |
| 41A | IOM | INT COUNTRY HOTEL/CAR PARK/PEOPLE CARRIER<br>TINA BITES CASS | | Night | 1/8 pgs. | 1, 25 |
| 41B | IOM | EXT COUNTRY HOTEL/CAR PARK<br>TINA GETS INTERRUPTED | | Night | 4/8 pgs. | 1, 2, 4, 6, 7, 8, 25, 26, 27 |
| 41C | IOM | EXT COUNTRY HOTEL/CAR PARK<br>THE DOOR IS FLUNG OPEN - ADAM IS NOT IMPRESSED - TINA | | Night | 4/8 pgs. | 1, 2, 4, 6, 7, 8, 25, 26, 27 |

**--- END OF DAY 26 -- Thu, Oct 9, 2003 -- 4 pgs.**

**SLEEP DAY AFTER NIGHT SHOOT**

**--- END OF DAY 27 -- Fri, Oct 10, 2003 -- pgs.**

Fig. 4. A page from a shooting schedule.

assistant director who is the next in the hierarchy of purely organisational jobs but whose principal responsibility really starts when actual shooting begins.

The more detailed the research at this stage and the more information that is provided by the director to his designer, production manager and assistant director and vice-versa, the smoother will be the actual production during shooting.

The designer (originally called the art director) is not only responsible for the actual design (see Figure 5 page 23) and commissioning of the building, painting and plastering of sets but, in consultation with the director, for the whole visual style including the furnishings and props, although the acquisition of these various elements either by making, purchasing or hiring, ultimately is the responsibility of individual craftsmen like carpenters, painters, plasterers, scenic artists and property men.

As these parts of the jigsaw begin to take shape, so further technicians join the team like the costume designer and the casting director. The former, especially if the story is not contemporary and may therefore mean that costumes have to be specially made, should certainly be engaged sufficiently early to allow time for this and subsequent fitting.

The casting director is not only responsible for finding suitable artistes for all parts, except the principals who may have already been agreed, but for arranging casting sessions for the director and, working either direct or through artists' agents, ensuring their availability and the negotiation of fees. The finalisation of this and the drawing up of contracts may however be done by the production manager and/or producer.

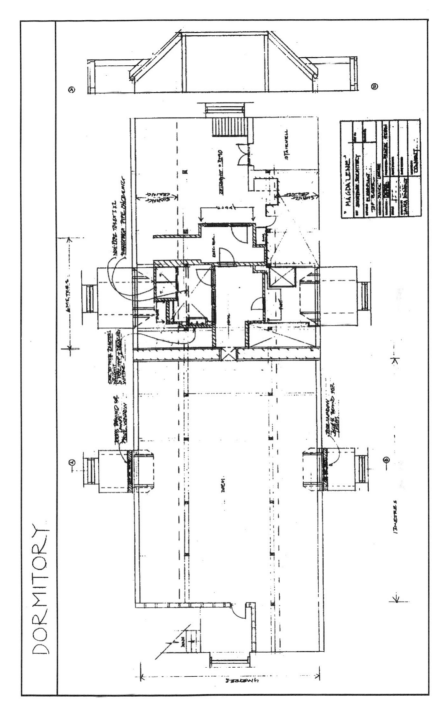

**Fig. 5. Set design.**

## Construction

So the tempo begins to increase and a head of construction will have been engaged and he will take on carpenters, plasterers and painters who will be building the sets designed by the art department which will by now have swelled to include assistant art directors and draughtsmen, set dressers and property buyers according to the size and complexity of the film.

At one time most studios had a permanent staff for the construction jobs and supplied the craftsmen plus riggers for erecting scaffolding and electricians for the production. Now it is more common for studios to operate as **'four wallers'**, that is just the buildings with very limited supporting facilities and for all the personnel to be engaged by the production company.

In parallel with this, the production manager will be engaging people for all the other departments: on the production side, second and third assistant directors, script supervisors (previously known as continuity) and additional accountants and bookkeepers.

## Camera crew

### *Lighting cameraman*

The camera crew consists of the lighting cameraman who might have already been signed up and gone on location surveys. He is one of the key creative people and hence may have been part of the package which attracted the finance, for he is not merely responsible for the technical excellence of the photography and for the individual members of his crew but the whole creative look of the picture, both interiors and exteriors.

## Camera operator

The next member of his team is the camera operator whose job is certainly to look through the viewfinder and operate the camera but also to follow the movement smoothly throughout the scene, framing each **set-up**. His knowledge and experience is especially useful to the director in advising him whilst scenes are being arranged and rehearsed as to correct eyelines for actor, size and angle of shots which will cut satisfactorily and smoothly with preceding and succeeding ones.

## Focus puller

The third member of the camera crew is the focus puller whose job is to keep the major point of interest of the scene sharp. This is not always as straightforward as it sounds, for with complicated scenes involving elaborate camera movement and moves by actors, constant change of focus may be required and this has to be done unobtrusively unless some deliberate shock is required.

## Clapper/loader

Next is the clapper/loader, once known as the clapper boy whose job must have been guyed more than any other in the film industry. On his board he marks the slate number, a term dating back to silent days when these numbers were indeed marked in chalk on a slate. This number starts at '1' on the first day of shooting and proceeds numerically to the end of the production. It bears no relation to the scene number in the script for it might well happen, for whatever reason, that the very first scene to be photographed on the first day of production might be the last scene in the script. Alongside the slate number is the take number recording the number of times each scene is repeated until the director and other technicians are satisfied.

When the camera is running at the right speed at the beginning of each shot, he is then told to 'mark it', shouts out the slate and take number and brings the top hinged part of the clapper board down to the bottom with a resounding crack and then exits as fast as possible. The reason for this operation will be explained when the editing procedure is reached.

The clapper/loader is also responsible for loading magazines with unexposed negative film, fixing these on to the camera and ensuring that all the working parts are clean and working satisfactorily. He also logs on negative report sheets (see Figure 6 page 27) the footage and particulars of each day's work which will provide information to the laboratory who will process the exposed negative, to the cutting room who will be editing the film and to the production office who will keep an eye on the amount of film stock being consumed.

At the end of each day, he will have to unload in a darkroom or changing bag the exposed film, put it in sealed and labelled cans with the negative report sheets and arrange for it to be sent to the laboratory for developing and printing.

## Grip

The next member of the camera crew is a **grip** who is responsible for erecting, transporting and operating whatever type of device is called for to move the camera in the shot. This could be a very simple trolley (called confusingly a **dolly**) on rubber wheels for use on a smooth surface or on tracks laid specially. There are many variations leading up from this in size

**J·D·C**

LONDON 01-903 7933

| CONTINUED FROM SHEET No. 144401 | SHEET NUMBER 2 | CONTINUED ON SHEET No. 14403 |
|---|---|---|

THE SHEET NUMBERS MUST BE QUOTED ON ALL DELIVERY NOTES, INVOICES AND OTHER COMMUNICATIONS RELATING THERETO

PRODUCING COMPANY  MERCHANT IVORY      STUDIOS OR LOCATION  DEVEN'S HOUSE.

PRODUCTION  IN CUSTODY                      PRODUCTION No.

DIRECTOR  ISMAIL MERCHANT  CAMERAMAN  LARRY PIZER  DATE 18.1

STATE IF COLOUR OR B & W  COLOUR  **PICTURE NEGATIVE REPORT**

ORDER TO                                                        LABORATORIES

STOCK AND CODE No.  FUJI 125

LABORATORY INSTRUCTIONS RE INVOICING, DELIVERY, ETC.

CAMERA AND NUMBER  ARRI BL III

EMULSION AND ROLL No.  417-006

CAMERA OPERATOR  RAJESH JOSHI

| MAG. No. | LENGTH LOADED | SLATE No. | TAKE No. | COUNTER READING | TAKE LENGTH | 'P' for Print | COL'R | LENS F/L & STOP | ESSENTIAL INFORMATION Colour description of scene, filter and/or diffusion used. Day, night or other effects. | CAN No. |
|---|---|---|---|---|---|---|---|---|---|---|
| 3 125 | 1000 | 1/4 | 1 | 172-189 | 17' | P | | 8 | Neena returning from main door, through grille. Exit frame R. 32mm | 3 |
| | | | 2 | 189-209 | 20' | P | | 8 | | |
| | | | C H A N G E | | | | | | | |
| 2 250 J | 1000 | 1/5 | 1 | 00-29 | 29' | – | | 4.5 | One & Curtain, exit frame R. 35 mm | 2 |
| | | | 2 | 29-49 | 20' | P | | 4.5 | | |
| 2 250 J | 1000 | 1/6 | 1 | 49-168 | 119' | P | | 4.8 | Neena giving Om breakfast 38 mm | 2 |
| | | | 2 | 168-286 | 118 | P | | 4.8 | | |
| 2 250 J | 1000 | 1/7 | 1 | 285-388 | 103' | | | 4.8 | CU Om lwi 50 mm. | 2 |
| | | | 2 | 388-485 | 97' | P | | | | |
| | | | 3 | 485-586 | 101' | P | | | | |
| 2 250 D | 1000 | 1/8 | 1 | 586-670 | 104' | P | | 4+ | CU Neena Gupta SOFT 50 mm | 2 |
| | | | 2 | 670-780 | 110' | | | | | |
| | | | 3 | | | | | | | |
| | | | C H A N G E | | | | | | | |

FOR OFFICE USE ONLY

| | | | | TOTAL CANS |
|---|---|---|---|---|
| TOTAL EXPOSED | TOTAL EXPOSED | TOTAL PRINTED | TOTAL FOOTAGE PREVIOUSLY DRAWN | |
| SHORT ENDS | HELD OR NOT SENT | | FOOTAGE DRAWN TODAY | |
| WASTE | TOTAL DEVELOPED | | PREVIOUSLY EXPOSED | |
| FOOTAGE LOADED | SIGNED: | | EXPOSED TODAY | |

Fig. 6. Negative report sheet.

and complexity according to the camera movement required by the director. These are called jibs, velocilators and cranes and may be operated manually or mechanically or a combination of both but with one common aim, to produce a completely smooth and unobtrusive movement of the camera.

The grip is responsible for packing, unpacking and carrying all this and the bulk of the camera equipment and if it is being transported in one or more vehicles may double as driver.

### VT operator

A more recent addition to the camera crew, responsible for operating the video assist and for recording and playing back the tape of rehearsals and takes through the director's monitor.

## Sound crew

The next element in the production team is the sound crew, consisting of a sound recordist who operates a " tape recorder and is responsible for the overall quality and balance of the sound. He is assisted by a boom operator who ensures that the microphones are in a position for recording the best quality sound. Microphones, which may be radio mikes, are normally mounted on a boom which may vary from a fairly basic type of extending arm to a more elaborate device with pulleys for moving it in any direction. The skill of the job is in following the action so that the microphone favours the actor who is speaking, whilst at the same time keeping it clear of the lighting and the possibility of causing a shadow or even intruding into the picture area. A close liaison with the camera operator is therefore required as more than one mike may be involved plus radio or chest mikes.

Like the clapper/loader, the boom operator is also responsible at the end of each day for packing up and labelling the rolls of " tape and filling in sound report sheets (see Figure 7 page 30). These rolls of tape are then sent to a sound studio for transfer to 35mm sprocketed magnetic tape for use in the cutting room.

## Other production crew

So much for the principal technicians on the production side. But with the start date of the schedule approaching, there are still a great many technicians and craftspeople to be lined up so that all is ready for that magical first day of shooting.

Costume fittings have to be arranged and wardrobe made ready, props, furnishings and drapes may still have to be purchased or hired, publicity to be arranged through a unit publicist or a company sub-contracted to handle the publicity for this particular film. Make-up, hairdresser, wardrobe and, if required on location, transport and catering have to be signed up.

Special effects may be called for: that is the supply of the simplest canister to provide smoke, to the arrangement of the most complicated battle scenes with explosions and gunfire; from the wonders of digital computerised devices to make Batman fly, to the painting of glass shots for creating exotic background to be merged optically in the laboratories or digitally with scenes photographed in more mundane studio or location situations. All these and many more are the province of the special effects supervisor and his team and all require forward planning if some element of their craft is included in the script.

| | | SOUND REPORT | | | |
|---|---|---|---|---|---|

| PROD CO. | PRODUCTION | EPISODE | JOB NUMBER | RECORDIST | DATE |
|---|---|---|---|---|---|
| SAMUELSON PICTURES | "YOU DON'T HAVE TO SAY YOU LOVE ME" | THE HOTEL | N/A | HAIR/ LAX | 9/10/03 |

| RECORDER | SYNC SYSTEM | SPEED | FRAME RATE | GAUGE | STOCK | TRACK DESIGNATION |
|---|---|---|---|---|---|---|
| FOSTEX PD-4 | NEO PILOT 50 60 FM PILOT TIMECODE 24, 25, 29.97, 29.97DF, 30 | 3¾ 7½ 15 | 24 (25) 29.97 30 | 16mm (35mm) | HHb | TRACK 1 TRACK 2 |

| ROLL | SLATE | TAKE LENGTHS, PRINT CIRCLE TAKES ONLY | | | | | | | | | | |
|---|---|---|---|---|---|---|---|---|---|---|---|---|
| | | 1 | 2 | 3 | 4 | 5 | 6 | 7 | 8 | 9 | 10 | REMARKS |
| 33 | 267 Ⓐ | ✓ | ✓AFS | ✓ | Ⓥ | Ⓥ | | | | | | |
| | Ⓑ | ✓ | ✓AFS | ✓ | Ⓥ | Ⓥ | | | | | | |
| | 268 Ⓐ | Ⓥ | | | | | | | | | | |
| | Ⓑ | Ⓥ | | | | | | | | | | |
| | 269 | ✓ | Ⓥ | ✓ | ✓ | Ⓥ | | | | | | |
| | 270 | ✓ | ✓ | ✓ | ✓ | Ⓥ | | | | | | |
| | 271 | ✓ | ✓ | ✓ | Ⓥ | Ⓥ | | | | | | |
| | 272 | ✓ | ✓ | ✓ | ✓ | ✓ | ✓AFS | Ⓥ | | | | ~~~~~~~~~~~ |
| | 273 | Ⓥ | Ⓥ | | | | | | | | | TWIN TRACK |
| | 274 Ⓐ | Ⓥ | Ⓥ | | | | | | | | | TWIN TRACK |
| | Ⓑ | Ⓥ | Ⓥ | | | | | | | | | GUSTY WIND. BETTER ON 2ND AND 3RD TAKES. |
| | 275 | ✓ | Ⓥ | Ⓥ | | | | | | | | |
| | | WILD TRACK - DIALOGUE FROM SC. 39 (SLATE 275) | | | | | | | | | | |
| | 276 | Ⓥ | Ⓥ | Ⓥ | | | | | | | | |
| | 277 | Ⓥ | Ⓥ | | | | | | | | | |
| | 278 | Ⓥ | | | | | | | | | | |
| | | | | | | | | | | | | |
| | | | | | | | | | | | | |
| | | | | | | | | | | | | |
| | | | | | | | | | | | | |
| | | | | | | | | | | | | |

| SPECIAL INSTRUCTIONS TO TRANSFER SUITE |
|---|
| |
| |
| |
| |

Fig. 7. Sound report sheet.

So let us assume that the first day of shooting and the complete schedule that follows has been fixed. The production office must now issue **call sheets** (see Figure 8 page 33) and if a location shoot is involved a movement order (see Figure 9) as well.

## A TYPICAL DAY'S WORK

By now you will have some idea of the roles of the various departments that make up a feature film unit, so let us move forward and see what happens in a typical day's work.

### The start of shooting

According to the call sheet, let's say the call is 8.30am on A stage at the studio. Shooting is scheduled for the sitting room of ...'s house, scenes ... to ... Make up, hairdressing, wardrobe and the relevant artists will have been called earlier so that they will be ready to start rehearsals as soon as possible after 8.30am. The director with the lighting cameraman, the camera operator and the artist can start to 'choreograph' the scene, working out the camera movement, dialogue and action so that the lighting cameraman can tell the **gaffer** or chief electrician how he wants the lights placed. As soon as the scene is roughly mapped out, the grip can lay tracks if necessary and be getting the camera on to the dolly or crane, the focus puller can start checking the various changes in focus throughout the shot and the sound crew can sort out the best positions for the microphones and boom.

The lighting may be the longest part of all this and, if very complicated, stand ins for the principals may be used to avoid the artists getting too hot and tired. Equally, the director may

## YOU DON'T HAVE TO (I.O.M) LIMITED
## "YOU DON'T HAVE TO SAY YOU LOVE ME"
### Call Sheet No.1  SUNDAY 7th SEPTEMBER 2003

EXECUTIVE PRODUCERS: SALLY CAPLAN, STEVE CHRISTIAN, DAVID KOSSE, DONALD STARR, DANIEL TAYLOR

| | | | |
|---|---|---|---|
| PRODUCERS: | MARC SAMUELSON, PETER SAMUELSON | UNIT CALL | 08:00 |
| DIRECTOR: | SIMON SHORE | Breakfast From | 07:15 |

**UNIT MOBILES:**

| | | |
|---|---|---|
| Lee Ruette  (Line Producer) | 07740 306 656 | **Production Office:** |
| Karen McLuskey (Co-Ordinator) | 07771 593 696 | Container City 1, |
| Trevor Kaye (Second Assistant Director) | 07977 988 443 | Trinity Buoy Wharf |
| Matt Steinman (Location Manager) | 07802 826 806 | 64 Orchard Place |
| Chris White (Unit Manager) | 07976 290 915 | London |
| | | E14 OJW |
| Sunrise: **06:23**    Sunset: **19:32** | | ☎: 020 7093 3131  FAX:  020 7093 3140 |

WEATHER: Windy day, brightening after lunch.

Minibus (1) to leave Production office at 07:00 for Unit Base then work to A.D's instructions.
Minibus (2) service crew & extras from Unit base to set.

| | |
|---|---|
| LOCATION | THE BRASSERIE ROCQUE, BROADGATE CIRCLE, EC2, |
| UNIT BASE | FINSBURY SQUARE, LONDON EC2, |

**NO CAMERAS ON SET WITHOUT PRIOR CONSULTATION WITH PRODUCTION OFFICE****
**PLEASE ENSURE YOU HAVE A COPY OF THE COMPANIES SAFETY & CONTROL CODE, RELATING TO FILMING, THEY ARE BEING GIVEN OUT BY RACHEL (RUNNER)****
**WE ARE LOOKING FOR FAMILY & FRIENDS TO APPEAR AS EXTRAS (GRATIS) THROUGHOUT THE SHOOT.  FOR DETAILS PLEASE CALL EMILY IN THE PRODUCTION OFFICE., IN PARTICULAR WHEN WE SHOOT SCENE 50 RUB-A-DUB – 15/09 – THANK YOU****

| SC | D/N | SETS | CAST | PAGES |
|---|---|---|---|---|
| | | LINE UP SCENES 16 & 17 then shoot: | | |
| 16 | D2 | EXT – RESTAURANT – CANARY WHARF | 2 | 1/8 |
| | | Incongruous Dylan rides through Canary Wharf | | |
| 16A | D2 | EXT – RESTAURANT – CANARY WHARF | 2 | 1/8 |
| | | Dylan arrives at the restaurant | | |
| 17 | D2 | INT – RESTAURANT – DINING AREA | 2,14 | 1 5/8 |
| | | Dylan asks how Johnny got on – " Errand Boy??" | | |
| 18 | D2 | EXT – RESTAURANT – CANARY WHARF | 2,14,15 | 1 3/8 |
| | | Johnny gets the job, Smitten Dylan meets Clare | | |
| | | STAND BY SCENE: | | |
| .48pt To Start | D8 | I/E – RESTAURANT – CANARY WHARF | 2,6,15 | 7/8 |
| | | Dylan & Claire chat on way out of Restaurant | | |
| | | | TOTAL PAGES | 4 1/8 |

| ARTISTE | | CHARACTER | P/UP | W/R | M/UP | L/U | O/S |
|---|---|---|---|---|---|---|---|
| 2 | JIMI MISTRY | DYLAN | 06:35 | 07:00 | 07:30 | 08:00 | 08:00 |
| 14 | GEORGE IRVING | MONTGOMERY | 07:00 | After L/U | After L/U | 08:00 | As Req |
| 15 | NINA YOUNG | CLAIRE | 10:00 | 10:30 | 11:00 | As Req | 12:00 |
| 6 | DANNY NUSSBAUM | JOHNNY | 12:00 | 14:00 | 14:30 | As Req | 15:00 |
| **CROWD** | | | | | | | |
| | 13 x City Types | C/O Another Face | | | 07:30 | Sc 16,16A,18 | |
| | 1 x Window Cleaner | C/O Another Face | | | 07:30 | Sc 16,16A,18 | |
| | 1 x Pierre the Chef | C/O Henry Tomlinson | | | 07:30 | Sc 17,48pt | |
| | 2 x Waiters | C/O Locations | | | 07:30 | Sc 17,48pt | |
| **STAND INS** | | | | | | | |
| | Alistair Johns | FOR UTILITY | | | 07:30 | | |
| | Ian Warwicker | FOR UTILITY | | | 07:30 | | |

Fig. 8. Call sheet.

32

| ACTION VEHICLES | As per to include Dylan's Cycle on set for Unit call |
|---|---|
| CAMERA | As per Mike Fox. |
| ELECTRICAL | As per Terry Hunt |
| ART DEPT/PROPS | As per Mark Leese to include coffee, paperwork, Bike chain, Claire's briefcase, Window cleaners bucket. |
| GRIPS | As per James Holloway |
| SOUND | As per Mike Lax to include a meeting either at lunchtime or in downtime to discuss technical aspects Playback Scene 50 jazz at the Rub-a-Dub with Henry, Simon & Lee. |
| COSTUMES | As per Sarah Burns |
| MAKE-UP/HAIR | As per Pam Haddock |
| CONSTRUCTION | As per Martin Streeter |
| UNIT NOTE: | **Please note Gavin (10) will now be in Scene 1a as per advanced schedule for 08/09, Vicky (5) will not appear in Scenes 1A, Kate (3) will not appear in scene 64 – 16/09.** |
| MEDICAL | Michael Prior (Unit Nurse) 07782 131 347 to be on call from unit call |
| RUSHES | To be handed to Minibus driver on wrap for delivery to Delux (London) contact Paul Dray 01895 833 617 |

| CATERING c/o WOODHALL'S |
|---|
| Breakfast from 07:15 @ Unit Base for 80 people<br>lunch from approx. 13:00 and at Unit Base 80 people<br>Afternoon tea, Sandwiches and cakes @ 16:00 on location for 80 people<br>Tea, Coffee and refreshments available all day please |

| FACILITIES c/o MOVIE MAKERS c/o Tom Cheate mob 07815 084 963 | | | UP & RUNNING FOR 06:30 |
|---|---|---|---|
| To include: | 1 x Make-up Bus | 1 x Costume Truck | 2 x 3 positions | 1 x 2 Position |
| | 1 x Production Office | 1 x Honey Wagon | 1 x Dining bus | |

| TRANSPORT c/o Set Wheels | | | | |
|---|---|---|---|---|
| **ARTISTE** | **PICK UP** | **FROM** | **TO** | **DRIVER** |
| (2) JIMI MISTRY then | 06:35 | Home | UNIT BASE | Steve Rogers – People Carrier 07932 165664 |
| (6) DANNY NUSSBAUM | 12:00 | Home | | |
| (14) GEORGE IRVING | 07:00 | Home | UNIT BASE | David Grose – People Carrier 07973 835 142 |
| (15) NINA YOUNG | 10:00 | Home | STAND BY AT UNIT BASE THEN PICK UP NINA YOUNG | Colin Griffin – People Carrier 07710 085 997 |
| SIMON SHORE | 06:45 | Home | UNIT BASE | Mike Billemore 07967 714 175 |

| ADVANCE SCHEDULE | | Monday 8th September 2003 | UNIT CALL | 08:00 – 19:00 |
|---|---|---|---|---|
| SC | D/N | SETS | CAST | PAGES |
| 1 | D | EXT - FOOTBAL PITCH (1) | 4,7,18 | 2/8 |
| | | B/CU Football. Joe adjusts the position on the penalty spot. | | |
| 1A | D | EXT – FOOTBALL PITCH (1) | 1,2,3,4,6,7,8,9,10,18 | 1/8 |
| | | Billy coaches in goal. He concentrates hard, Snarls | | |
| 1B | D | EXT – FOOTBALL PITCH (1) | 4,7,18 | 4/8 |
| | | Adam collecting Corner flags, Joe strikes the ball. | | |
| 2 | D | EXT – FOOTBALL PITCH (1) | 1,2,3,4,6,7,8,9,10 | 3/8 |
| | | The team chant & horseplay around | | |
| 3 | D | EXT – FOOTBALL PITCH (1) | 1,2,3,4,6,7,8,9,10,18 | 1 4/8 |
| | | Adam wolf whistles Kate-"You don't have to say you love me" | | |
| | | | **TOTAL PAGES** | **2 6/8** |
| | | | Henry Tomlinson – Assistant Director | |

**Fig. 8. Call sheet (continued).**

---

3. TRANSPORT. Taxi to P/up JANET MCTEER from the County Hotel at 0630 hrs and transport to location.

Taxi to P/up DAVID OLIVER at TBA and convey to Tyne Tees Television for 0700 hrs.

Taxi to P/up KELLY ANN GREEENHALGH at 0630 hrs and convey to Tyne Tees for 0700 hrs.

Taxi to P/up BRADLEY MALCOLM at TBA and convey to Tyne Tees for 0700 hrs.

GWEN DORAN O/T TO T.T.T. for 0700 hrs.

LYN DOYGLAS O/TtTO T.T.T. for 0700 hrs.

Mini-bus 1. Jim to pick up glass artist and operators from the County Hotel at 0645 hrs and then to T.T.T. to pick up Artistes 0700 hrs then to proceed to location.

CREW. Transport. Mini-bus 2. (Martin) to P/up crew from County Hotel at 0745 hrs and then to T.T.T. to pick up remainder of crew.

N.B. Mini bus to LEAVE at 0800 hrs sharp and convey to location.

---

**Fig. 9. Movement order.**

use this time to rehearse elsewhere the artists' moves and delivery of dialogue.

## Rehearsal

So all is ready and the first assistant director calls for 'Quiet please – standby for rehearsal!' Then, 'Action!' from the director, and the first rehearsal is under way. Observations are sought by the director from the camera operator who may in turn discuss the key moments for the change of focus with the focus puller. The lighting cameraman may have noticed light adjustments that are necessary, the sound recordist (who may have recorded the rehearsal) will discuss with the boom swinger the placing of the mikes and the script supervisor may have a point of continuity which did not relate to a previous or subsequent shot which may have to be done weeks later.

And, of course, most importantly, the director will be judging the performances of the artists. This will be made easier if he has the benefit of a TV monitor by the camera.

## The first shot in the can

So the next stage is reached when the first assistant director is able to say 'Standby for a take – everybody quiet please.' Then comes his order 'turn over' which is the signal to the sound recordist to switch on the tape recorder and report 'running' and for the camera operator to switch on the camera and when it is up to the required speed to report 'speed' at which the first assistant director orders 'mark it' to the clapper/loader. This gives him the cue to get in with the clapper board, shouting out the slate and take number, bring the hinged portion down with a resounding clap and exit. Only then can the director order 'action' and the scene proceed up to the time he orders 'cut' which is the order for the camera and sound to be switched off.

Observations are then sought from camera and sound crews and the director decides whether to go for another take. If so, the first assistant director orders, 'Once more please – first positions,' and the whole process is repeated until everybody is satisfied with the result. The director then decides which of the various takes he would like printed and this information is given to the camera and sound crews so that they can make a note on their respective report sheets.

As a rule, all picture negative is developed at the laboratories and only those shots and takes indicated are printed. In the case of sound, all the " master tape is stored but again, only the shots and takes indicated are transferred to 35mm sprocketed tape.

And so the day proceeds with the first assistant director keeping an eye on the clock and diplomatically urging everybody forward to ensure that the day's schedule is adhered to. The normal working day is 8.30am to 6.30pm (maybe even longer) and assuming all has gone well, the last order that the first assistant will give is, 'It's a **wrap**'.

## After a wrap

But this is not the end of the day's work for many of the unit. The clapper/loader has to unload the magazines and put the exposed film into cans, fill in the report sheets and arrange transport to the laboratory. Similarly, the boom swinger has to label up the " tape and arrange for its transfer. The grip has to pack away the camera equipment and all other departments will be making sure that all is ready for the next day's work. The script supervisor will be typing up the continuity sheets (see Figure 10 page 37) which provide information on every shot completed that day and are sent to the production office and the cutting room.

The director will certainly be discussing with the first assistant, and perhaps the producer and production manager, the next scenes to be shot and there might at the end of the day be a rushes screening. **Rushes** (or in the US dailies) is the term for the film and sound used during the day, processed or transferred overnight, assembled by the editor and his crew and viewed by all concerned.

Time may be set aside during the lunch break or in the evenings and opinions vary as to who should attend these rushes viewing sessions. The producer, director and editor of course. The lighting cameraman and sound recordist almost certainly. The remainder of the crew and artists? This is where individual directors and producers have differing ideas. If, as a newcomer, it is possible to attend rushes, there is a lot to be

DAILY CONTINUITY REPORT

| | | | Script Number |
|---|---|---|---|
| Production: | MAURICE | | ID |
| | | | Slate Number |
| Date | 13.11 | | 355 |
| set: | EXT. BEACH | | |

| CAMERA | SET UP 65/55mm. 35/8' T.5.85 | | Sync Mute Night Day |
|---|---|---|---|

| Take | 1 | 2 | 3 | 4 | 5 | 6 | 7 | 8 | 9 | 0 |
|---|---|---|---|---|---|---|---|---|---|---|
| Print | cut | poss | fluff | poss | PT | cut | cut | fluff | PT | |
| Reason n.g. | | (nvg cam) | (ok for cam) | | | | | (good for cam) | | |
| Timing | | | | | | | | | 18s | |

MS. DUCIE & MAURICE in dunes, r/1 - talking about next school. MAURICE says 'I'm a boy'./ They exit r/l (to beach).

Shooting towards dunes.

V.O. DUCIE: SPLENDID. SPLENDID. (enters r/l MAURICE following). WHAT DID MR ABRAHAMS SAY. TOLD YOU YOU WERE A MISERABLE SINNER I HOPE.

They continue f.g. of high dune to f.g.

MAURICE : (stop)   MR ABRAHAMS SAID I AM NEVER TO DO ANYTHING I WOULD BE ASHAMED TO HAVE MY MOTHER SEE ME DO (Alt. T5 - ASHAMED TO DO IN FRONT OF MY MOTHER) HE SAID MY NEXT SCHOOL WILL BE MORE LIKE THE WORLD.

DUCIE:   DID HE. DID HE (walks fwd) & WHAT'S THE WORLD LIKE DO YOU SUPPOSE. (he exits r/l - to beach).

MAURICE:   (following) I DON'T KNOW SIR. I'M A BOY. (he exits).

**Fig. 10. Continuity sheet.**

37

learned from seeing all the scenes as they come out of the camera and from hearing the observations of the principal creative people.

And so the daily or sometimes nightly schedule proceeds with all its dramas and problems, large and small, with attendant overtime and even with days where everything goes marvellously right and everybody gets home at not too ungodly an hour. Let's therefore leave the shooting side of the production and see what has been happening meanwhile in parallel on post-production.

## POST-PRODUCTION

NOTE: the following is a description of the traditional methods of editing on film. However, the introduction of non-linear digital editing systems such as Avid or Lightworks means that these methods are now increasingly being used throughout the world. See page 87, Commercials Post-Production, for digital editing procedures (including digital effects).

### Initial stages

By post-production is meant the assembling and editing of picture and sound, recording of music, creation, re-recording and mixing of sound tracks, preparing and making graphics for titles and the processing of the film in the laboratory from the developing and printing of the rushes to the making of the final prints for release to cinemas.

At the end of the day's shooting, the exposed picture negative will have been developed and printed overnight by the laboratory. The negative remains at the laboratory and the

## "COTTON MARY"
### DAILY PRODUCTION REPORT

DATE : Thursday, Dec 31st, 1998

**MERCHANT IVORY PRODUCTIONS**   Director: Ismail Merchant

| START DATE: | 12/14/98 | SET LOCATION | | | SCENE NUMBERS | | |
|---|---|---|---|---|---|---|---|
| FINISH DATE: | 02/11/98 | THAKUR HOUSE | | | COMPLETED: 86A, 86, 47, 47A, 1A, 37 | | |
| ESTIMATED DAYS: | 45 | 1/15 DUTCH CEMETERY ROAD | | | | | |
| DAYS TO DATE: | 15 | | | | PART: | | |
| REMAINING DAYS: | 30 | | | | | | |
| DAYS OVER: | 00 | | | | | | |

| DIARY | | SET-UPS | | SCRIPT INFORMATION | | | |
|---|---|---|---|---|---|---|---|
| CALL TIME: | 08:00AM | PREVIOUS: 133 | | PAGES TODAY: | 5 | TIME TODAY: | 6'17 |
| 1ST SHOT: | 09:30AM | TODAY: 13 | | TOTAL PAGES: | 44 2/8 | TOTAL TIME: | 53'11 |
| MEAL BREAK: | 13:10PM | TOTAL: 146 | | EXTRA SCENES: | 00 | PAGES & TIME: | |
| UNIT DISMISED: | 20:06PM | SLATE #'S: 86A/4-7, 86/1-2 | | REYAKES: | 00 | PAGES & TIME: | |
| HOURS ON SET: | 12hr 06m | 47/1, 1A/1, 47A/1-4, 37/1 | | | | | |

| ACTION PROPS / EFX / ANIMALS | ADDTL. EQUIPMENT / FACILITIES | |
|---|---|---|
| Piles of white sheets, Lily's perfumes | | |
| Lily's clothes, Tea cup | | |
| Photo of Lily in England | | |

| CAST | | CALLED | DISMISSED | EXTRAS | |
|---|---|---|---|---|---|
| MADHUR JAFFREY | | 08:00AM | 18:00PM | | |
| GRETA SCACCHI | | 07:30PM | 20:00PM | | |
| LAURA LUMLEY | | 08:00AM | 11:25AM | N/A | |
| PRAYAG RAAJ | | 15:45PM | 16:45PM | | |
| SAKINA JAFFREY | | 10:00AM | 18:00PM | | |
| JAMES WILBY | | 11:00AM | 18:00PM | | |
| VIREN SAXENA | | 07:30AM | 10:45AM | | |
| | | | | CATERING FIGURES: | 55 |

| FILM FOOTAGES | | | | | | SOUND STOCK | |
|---|---|---|---|---|---|---|---|
| | LOADED | PRINTED | EXPOSED | WASTE | S / ENDS | | LOADED |
| PREVIOUSLY: | 51,710 | 25,520 | 41,622 | 138 | 9,860 | PREVIOUSLY: | 55 |
| TODAY: | 4,750 | 3,690 | 4,350 | 0 | 400 | TODAY: | 6 |
| TO DATE: | 56,460 | 29,210 | 45,972 | 138 | 10,260 | TO DATE: | 61 |

**NOTES:**   SCENE #86A = 3'02, #86 = 38", #47 = 20", #47A = 1'15, #1A = 21", #37 = 40"

One hour delay in the am due to denied access to the location.

Added additional 360ft to be printed from footage shot Dec 30th, 1998. This is refelected in the total #'s.

HAPPY NEW YEAR !

We're one third through the shoot !

John P. Scholz
Production Manager

## Fig. 11. Daily production report.

TECHNICOLOR LTD FILM SERVICES Rush Print Viewing Report (TEL: 0181-759-5432, FAX: 0181-759-5016)

| Date 02/09/99 | Roll No. 44921_ANEG | Prod ID No 101098 | Production COTTON MARY | Aug 26. 1999 14:58:02 |
|---|---|---|---|---|
| Production Company MERCHANT IVORY | | Bill To PROD CO | Customer Order No. LOG 136399 TO 401 | Photo Date 4FEB99 |

| Mat'l Submtd: FUJI 8532 | Cameraman: PIERRE L"HOMME | |
|---|---|---|
| Develped Date/time: 9/2 | Printed By: | |
| Del To: NABD............... | Print Mach#: | Time: : |
| | Assembled By: CLIFF | |
| Matl Printed: 35MM COL PRINT | Remarks: #84982-83-84 RB38 | |
| Del Add 1. | | |
| Del Add 2. | TOTAL NEG 1360FT | FEATURE |
| Del Add 3. | Neg Ftg x # Prts = Total Footage 837 x 1 = 837 | |

| Scn Pos | Slate Scene-Take | Lights YY CC HH EV | KeyKode | PDC Feet+Fr | Scene Description | Cam. Roll | Scn Len Feet+Fr |
|---|---|---|---|---|---|---|---|
| 1 | LDR-* | 26 26 26 26 | | 0000+00 | X-FRAME | | 0009+04 |
| 2 | 78/1-2 | 30 30 37 32 | FN 71 6881 5816 | 0009+04 | | 99 | 0135+09 |
| 3 | 78/2-1 | 31 32 39 34 | FN 71 6881 5952 | 0144+13 | | 99 | 0068+04 |
| 4 | 78/2-2 | 31 32 39 34 | FN 71 6881 6020 | 0213+01 | | 99 | 0064+01 |
| 5 | 78/2-3 | 31 32 39 34 | FN 71 6881 6084 | 0277+02 | | 99 | 0075+00 |
| 6 | 78/3-1 | 31 32 39 34 | FN 71 6881 6159 | 0352+02 | | 99 | 0051+00 |
| 7 | 78/3-2 | 31 32 39 34 | FN 71 6881 6210 | 0403+02 | | 99 | 0029+01 |
| 8 | 78/3-3 | 31 32 39 34 | FN 71 6881 6239 | 0432+03 | | 99 | 0032+11 |
| 9 | 19/1-3 | 25 34 35 31 | FN 32 1403 2356 | 0464+14 | X | 41AB | 0052+15 |
| 10 | 19/1-4 | 25 34 35 31 | FN 32 1403 2409 | 0517+13 | X | 41AB | 0056+14 |
| 11 | 19/1-5 | 25 34 35 31 | FN 32 1403 2466 | 0574+11 | X | 41AB | 0061+11 |
| 12 | 20/1-2 | 29 40 42 37 | FN 71 6881 6323 | 0636+06 | X | 99A | 0039+09 |
| 13 | 20/1-3 | 29 40 42 37 | FN 71 6881 6363 | 0675+15 | X | 99A | 0043+04 |
| 14 | 20/2-3 | 22 35 37 31 | FN 71 6881 6657 | 0719+03 | X | 99A | 0112+03 |
| 15 | LDR-* | 26 26 26 26 | | 0831+06 | FOOT | | 0006+00 |

General Comments

Fig. 12. Laboratory report.

prints are despatched as early as possible to the cutting room. Somebody from the production unit, either the first assistant director or one of the camera crew will have already telephoned the contact at the lab for a rushes report. This is purely a technical report on the state of the negative, exposure, steadiness and so on. If there is anything doubtful, the editor will have also received a written report with the rushes prints and will have had a look himself and conferred with the director and producer as to whether it is necessary to consider a re-take.

Laboratories vary in how meticulous their technical observations can be and many a devastating report on a certain scene can turn out to be exaggerated and no cause for panic. But equally, real disasters may call for very quick decisions on the part of the producer as highly paid artists may have to be re-called and schedules re-arranged if re-takes due to technical faults prove necessary, although many faults can now be corrected digitally (see pages 123–125 computerised animation).

## Synching up the rushes

Let us assume that the report from the lab is 'all OK' and that the sound rushes, that is the 35mm sprocketed tape, have also been received by the cutting room. The first job of the assistant editors, first and/or second, is to 'synch up' the rushes. This is done by placing the print of the picture and the magnetic tape in a **synchroniser** which is a device for running two or more pieces of sprocketed film or tape in parallel on a cutting room bench. The assistant then has to find the relevant slate and take number on the picture and mark with a chinagraph pencil the exact frame where the hinged part of the clapper board meets the lower part. He then has to find on the magnetic tape, listening to the voice of the clapper/loader, the same slate and take number and the sound of the clap marking this exact frame also with the chinagraph. The picture and sound are then put into the synchroniser in parallel and are wound on to wire spools with two lengths of 'leader' at the front with parallel start marks for the projectionist to lace up when running the rushes. Start and synch marks for picture are marked ⊠ and sound ▯.

So each scene is joined on to the next, keeping each roll in synch throughout in the synchroniser and finally rewound so as to be ready for viewing by the unit.

After the rushes have been viewed, the picture and sound will be sent for numbering – that is the printing of the slate number and the cumulative footage down the side of the film and tape from the clapper board to the end of the scene. This is done so that however the film is subsequently cut and edited, the picture and sound can be put in the synchroniser matching the numbers and kept in synch. Studios may have their own numbering machines or special companies may offer this service.

After numbering, the rushes have to be logged in a notebook, writing the slate and take numbers with a short description of the scene, the 'edge' or 'key' numbers which are printed by the stock manufacturers and the newly printed 'rubber' numbers. This log book forms the basic filing system for the assistant editors and during the subsequent editing and re-editing process is absolutely essential for reference.

# 1 ALL IN THE GAME / DELANTERO    LOG SHEET

| SL: | KEY NO. | RUBBER NO. | LAB ROLL | SOUND ROLL | SC: |
|---|---|---|---|---|---|
| 135/4T1 | KK07 0368 4459-4511 | 135 4000- 060 | 6-8-93 155 | 246 | 35 |
| 135/4T3 | 4563- 4649 | 061 - 169 | | | |
| 135/4T4 | 4650-4696 | 170 - 227 | | ↓ | |
| 135/5T2 | 4736-4788 | 5000 - 061 | | 247 | |
| 135/5T3 | 4809- 4867 | 062 - 135 | | | |
| 135/5T5 | 8886- 8941 | 136 - 205 | | | |
| 135/6T2 | 8988 - 9036 | 6000- 055 | | | |
| 135/6T3 | 9037- 9085 | 056 - 116 | | | |
| 135/6T4 | 9788- 9838 | 117 - 180 | ↓ | ↓ | ↓ |
| | | | | | |
| 136/1T1A | KK07 0395 0218- 0278 | 136 A 1000 - 060 | 2-8-93 141 | 233 | 36 |
| 136/1T1B | 0374 1800- 1860 | B 1000 - 071 | ↓ | | |
| 136/1T2A | 0395 0299- | A 1072 - 170 | 141 | | |
| 136/1T2B | - 1959 | B 1072 - 187 | ↓ | | |
| 136/2T1A | 0363 - 0461 | A 2000 - 119 | 141 | | |
| 136/2T1B | 0374 1961 - 2094 | B 2000 - 163 | ↓ | ↓ | ↓ |
| | | | | | |
| 137/1T4 | KK07 0374 9295 - 9380 | 137 1000 - 126 | 2-8-93 141 | 232 | 37 |
| 137/1T5 | 9381 - 9488 | 127 - 261 | | | |
| 137/1T7 | 9529 - 9632 | 262 - 391 | | | |
| 137/1T10 | 9865 - 9971 | 392 - 525 | | | |
| 137/2T2 | 0013 - | 2000 - 039 | | | |
| 137/2T5 | 0395 0048 - 175 | 040 - 091 | | | |
| 137/2T6 | 176 - 0216 | 092 - 142 | ↓ | 233 | ↓ |

**Fig. 13. Cutting room logbook.**

## Breaking down the rushes

The next job is for the rolls of rushes to be broken down into their separate slate numbers. These are individually rolled up and put into tins or boxes clearly labelled for easy access.

It may become possible now for the editor to start assembling various sequences whilst the shooting is still in progress. The cutting room staff will have copies of the shooting script which can be cross referenced with the continuity sheets which will show the script number to which each slate number refers. The assembly of sequences is put together as far as possible in script order and gradually the film begins to take shape. The completed full rolls (approximately 1,000 feet of 35mm) of picture and sound are called the cutting copy and are labelled action cutting copy reel 1 and sound or dialogue cutting copy reel 1.

## Editing builds up

And so the reels build up as shooting proceeds and, in theory, it should be possible to have a rough assembly of the whole film very soon after the last day of shooting.

There may however be sections missing. For example, special effects shots, overseas establishing shots, sequences or shots which are being staged by a second unit under a second unit director and second unit cameraman and crew. Although some of these second unit shots may be purely routine, such as a car driving past camera, they may involve elaborate stunts employing stunt men with shots incorporating flying, ski-ing, underwater or falls or crashes. James Bond films are a good example of where the material from the second unit is every bit as important as that from the main unit.

The first assembly of a film is invariably too long but most editors and directors prefer to start that way and then reduce and tighten up sequences for this makes it easier to see where the film loses momentum and even whether some scenes or sequences might be removed altogether.

But this is where the editor's experience is invaluable to the director even if the editor's proposals for cutting and elimination may sometimes prove painful to the director who remembers the agonies he has gone through and even the time to complete a certain shot. But he will be well advised to heed the editor's advice with his more detached view of the film and, of course, his talent as an editor.

Conversely, for an editor to have the opportunity of examining the raw material from the start and of seeing where the director may have gone wrong, is very useful training for an editor with ambitions to direct.

Similarly, the job of assistant editor, although not requiring particularly creative skills but merely the ability to anticipate the requirements of the editor and operate a meticulous filing system, can provide useful opportunities to observe the skills of an editor as he builds up the pace and rhythm of a film.

## Power of editing

Much has been written about the power of editing from the early silent Russian films of Eisenstein to the techniques of David Lean. Suffice here to say that a good editor can certainly improve an actor's performance and enliven a routine script but cannot change radically a bad basic idea.

In spite of the growth in transferring film to tape or disc for editing (see Chapter 4, Documentaries), cutting on film still enables the editor to view sequences projected on a large screen in a viewing theatre. However, tape and disc editing allow faster access and the ability to try alternative cuts quickly but sequences can only be viewed on a monitor. So let's assume the editor is cutting on film.

## Technicalities of editing

The most common device for viewing film in a cutting room is called a **Steenbeck**. This enables the picture to be seen on a screen and can take one or more sound tracks laced up synchronously. Picture and sound can be run forwards or backwards, singly or together, fast or slowly, right down to viewing each frame of film individually. As with the assistant synching up the rushes initially, the editor uses a chinagraph pencil to mark the frame where he wishes to make the cut.

The spare material from the beginning and end of the scene is taken by the assistant, rolled up and marked with its slate and take number. All these unused pieces are put into boxes which are called cuts. The unused scenes are called spares.

It is here that the assistant needs to take care with the filing system for, as the editing proceeds, the editor may want to add to a scene previously cut and will expect the assistant to find the right piece straight away. Likewise if scenes get progressively shorter, the assistant must keep all the pieces carefully wrapped and labelled.

## The rough cut

When the whole film has been assembled and roughly edited, all the reels of cutting copy, action and sound, are called the rough cut. They are gradually fined down, emphases changed perhaps, sequences transposed or left out until both the editor and director are satisfied with the result so that they can arrange a screening to the producer of what may now be termed the fine cut. He may have useful suggestions to make, both because he has not been so intimately involved over such a long period and may spot immediately some part of the film which is unclear, dull or slow.

He may also have political points to consider, knowing the backers, investors or distributors. But he must perform his balancing act with the utmost tact, remembering that his first loyalty is to the film. Showings may have to be arranged to these other parties and it may be advisable to add more of the sound track for a rough cut screening, as the picture having been handled frequently in the cutting room can indeed look pretty rough, and with no music and scant sound effects at this stage still requires a lot of imagination on the part of the viewer. By moving forward a few steps, the film may look more polished and thus reassure a lay audience at these rough cut shows but should major changes be demanded, retreat can become more difficult and costly.

## The sound track

Assuming the film survives unscathed from these various screenings, the next stages of editing can proceed. The editor and director will start planning the sound track – the sections which will require music and the extent of the sound effects.

Here a dubbing editor with one or more assistants may take over the film and assume responsibility for this part of the operation right up to the stage of **dubbing** the film.

Dubbing in this context means the mixing together of all the sound tracks – dialogue, music and sound effects – at the right levels so that one sound does not drown out another but maximum dramatic impact is achieved by the volume of each sound. The final mix is then re-recorded on to magnetic tape and is called the final mixed or dubbed track.

The editor may be concerned with post-synching or **ADR** (automatic dialogue replacement) of parts of the film where location recording has proved to be of not high enough quality, due to background noise of traffic, aircraft, wind or other things outside the recordist's control.

This involves the assistant removing scenes from the cutting copy and making them into rolls or loops of picture and the sound track already recorded which may be called guide track. The picture sections are cued where the dialogue starts and finishes and the artists make a new recording of the dialogue matching the lip movements on the screen but now in perfect acoustic conditions of a recording theatre. The director will be present at these sessions for the artists will be giving virtually a fresh performance.

## Music

A composer will by now have been appointed and discussions of the type of music and the make-up and size of the orchestra will be considered. Budgetary constraints may be a factor here although sometimes the most effective scores have arisen out of small or unexpected combinations, the zither in *The Third Man* being a classic example. Electronically produced music, whilst certainly more economical than a 60 piece orchestra, can sometimes be just as effective.

The principal consideration in background music in films is that there are no rules. Extremely catchy music using a single instrument like the harmonica in *Genevieve* can work; a large orchestra or anything in between and highly abstract music can also work. All can equally fail miserably.

Once the music sections of the film have been agreed by the editor, director and composer, the assistant editor can then prepare music cue sheets (see Figure 14 page 50). These are lists starting with a description of the first shot of each section and measured in feet from zero. The footage of any particularly relevant point (an action or word of dialogue) within a scene may also be marked as the composer may want to punctuate this with a note or phrase of music.

When the composer has completed the score, he may try out sections on the director and editor by playing on a piano, but this is seldom satisfactory as it is hard to give an impression of the different instruments and orchestration. This is where the composer who produces his own electronic music has the advantage, for he can bring a cassette of music into the cutting room and run it roughly in synch with the picture. He can then return to his studio and make changes or additions.

## Music session

In the case of a composer using an orchestra, his next job is to get his score copied for each instrument and possibly for a fixer

1M12

| | |
|---|---|
| 00'36½" | Riah looks down at silk shirts. |
| 00'38" | Cut to corridor outside attic. |
| 00'39" | Candle appears followed by Miller – |
| 00'41" | and Riah. |
| 00'43½" | Riah dial. "I am grateful..." |
| 00'45½" | Miller continues dial. |
| 00'47.1/4" | Dial. ends "... long overdue." |
| 00'48" | They stop walking as Miller turns to Riah. |
| 00'49" | Miller dial. "Being able to help..." |
| 00'53" | "... such an obligation to you." (dial. pause) |
| 00'54" | Miller does a double take on Riah. |
| 00'56" | Riah smiles. |
| 00'57" | Riah starts to turn and move off. |
| 00'57.3/4" | Miller dial. "Riah..." |
| 00'58" | Riah turns her head back to listen. |
| 00'59" | Miller moves forward. |
| 01'00" | Miller stops and looks into her eyes. |
| 01'01" | Miller dial. "You know, sometimes..." |
| 01'04" | Dial. ends "... your daughter." <br> Riah and Miller continue looking at each other. |
| 01'06.1/4" | Riah finally moves her head away, smiles. |
| 01'07" | She turns to leave, Miller's eyes follow. |
| 01'08½" | Riah leaves frame. |
| 01'09½" | Miller makes a movement forward to watch her go. |
| 01'10½" | Cut to Riah on stairs, revealing Miller still <br> watching at the top. |
| 01'14½" | Begin fade to black. |
| 01'17" | Fade to black ends. |
| | (Caption "The Black Velvet Gown" will fade up.) |
| 01'20" | END OF PART ONE. |
| CUE ENDS | |

**Fig. 14. Music cue sheet.**

to be engaged. A fixer signs up the best instrumentalists available at the time that the music recording theatre has been booked for the music session.

Some composers conduct their own score and sometimes a conductor is employed. The fixer liaises with the production manager and the accountant over the rates to be paid to each individual musician which may include such extra items as doubling on two instruments, porterage and travelling. The Musicians' Union is highly organised and the schedule for music recording is very important to the producer for if it is exceeded by even one hour over the normal session of four hours, payment will have to be made to all the musicians for a further complete session.

The music recording will be attended by the producer, director and editor and the assistant will have marked or removed the various sections from the cutting copy. The first section of music from reel 1 is called 1M1, the second in reel 1, 1M2 and so on through the film. Each recording of each section is announced by the conductor or recordist '1M1 Take 1' and notes are made of the best takes as far as performance and fitting the synch points are concerned.

During the recording, the section of music is projected on a screen or monitor facing the conductor and the start of each section is cued in from zero with the accumulating footages also projected. Footages from the music cue sheet will appear where necessary on the conductor's score and it is up to him to regulate the tempo of the orchestra accordingly.

A copy of the score will also be with the recordist or recording engineer who also has the responsibility for placing the various microphones for the instruments in the studio. In making the recording, he will be aiming to get the best balance between the instruments in collaboration with the composer. In all probability, he will record each track separately and only after the session is completed will he mix the various tracks into one master music mix.

Other technicians in the recording studio are recording assistants to lace up and supervise the recording on tape of the various tracks and projectionists who are screening the music sections of the film. The various recorded sections of music are transferred to 35mm magnetic tape for the cutting room and all this has to be logged and filed by the assistant editor before being fitted synchronously against the cutting copy by the editor or dubbing editor.

## Sound effects

The dubbing editor will now be acquiring the sound effects for the film, either by arranging to have them specially recorded or by obtaining them from a library of sound effects.

Strangely, the recording of footsteps is one of the most laborious parts of this operation; footsteps recorded during production in a studio or on location are seldom sufficiently distinct, as the recordist has concentrated on the dialogue. Thus in exactly the same way as rolls were made up for post-synching dialogue, so are they prepared for recording footsteps. There are a few artists who specialise in the recording of footsteps and their experience can speed up enormously somewhat wearisome recording sessions in a studio. The artist arrives with a bag of assorted shoes and boots to match the characters on the screen and the studio provides a variety of surfaces like paving stones, gravel or wood.

## Dubbing the film

So the number of cans of sound tracks begins to increase, each track of each reel of cutting copy with its start mark and synchronised with the action cutting copy. And most importantly, clearly marked both on the leaders of the tapes and boxes or cans – reel 1 music 1, reel 1 FX 1, reel 1 FX 2 and so on. (**FX** is the traditional shortening of the word effects.) The reason for several sound tracks in parallel is that many sounds will be superimposed and each will have to have its own level in the final mix. If there are long sections of consistent background noise such as traffic or restaurant chatter, loops may be made up for these.

When all these tracks have been completed and laid, the assistants will prepare a dubbing cue sheet to assist the sound mixer in the dubbing theatre. These cue sheets are made up for each reel and show the footage of every sound – dialogue, music, sound effects – against descriptions of the picture with special sound punctuations marked. Often different tracks can be shown in different colours to make the chart clearer for the mixer.

The basic purpose of mixing or dubbing has already been described. And so the producer, director, editor, dubbing editor and assistants assemble in the dubbing theatre for one of the final processes in post-production.

The dubbing theatre is a viewing theatre equipped for running the picture with a great many tracks interlocked to run synchronously. Once laced up, they can be run forwards or backwards remaining in synch; when it was first introduced this system was given the name 'rock and roll'.

In the theatre, the dubbing mixer with one or more assistants, depending on the number of tracks, sit behind a mixing desk or console. Each track has its own fader and it is the mixer's job to regulate these at the right level to give the greatest creative mix to the sound track overall. The director and editors may have their own views as to what they have in mind for particular points in the film but both the technical and creative skills of the mixer should be paramount.

The lacing up and supervision of the picture and tracks require projectionists and the supervision of the recording calls for recording assistants.

If foreign language versions of the film are eventually to be made, a mix of the music and effects only, leaving out any dialogue or narration, may also be done. This track is called an M and E.

## Laboratory completion work

When the dubbing has been completed, provided the film is scheduled for a normal cinema release, the mixed magnetic track is transferred to optical negative film which is sent to the laboratory for developing.

Apart from the final work at the lab, there are only two other processes of post-production which concern the cutting room. The first is the design and photography of the titles and credits and these can be a mini-production in themselves, not only from the point of view of design but also with timing, synchronising with music, for example. They may incorporate complicated animation techniques and special effects and are often sub-contracted to companies who specialise in this sort of

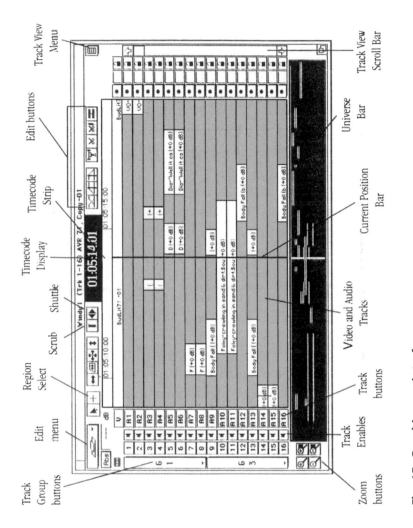

**Fig. 15. Graphic user interface
(equivalent of dubbing cue sheet used in linear editing).**

55

work. At their most basic, they can consist of computer generated or printed art work photographed on a **rostrum camera** (see Chapter 5 on Animation).

The second process is the ordering and making up of **opticals**. Opticals are fades in the picture, mixing from one scene to another (may be called dissolves) or any other device for transition between scenes other than a straight cut. At one time in feature films, a great variety of optical – vertical and horizontal wipes, hard or soft edge, irises, ripples and so on were used and laboratories published catalogues of the choice of these devices they could make. They have largely gone out of fashion now, except in trailers, although there has been a resurgence in two other areas – pop videos and television titles, where they are achieved in the video edit suite and not optically in the laboratory.

The optical process in the laboratory means re-photographing the two scenes of negative on to a duplicate negative which incorporates the effect required. A print of the finished optical is sent to the cutting room for cutting in to the **cutting copy** and a print of the titles is similarly cut in.

There may have to be a final show of the cutting copy with the mixed track to a variety of interested parties before the film can be sent to the laboratory for the last stage of post-production.

## Negative cutting and grading

The negative of the film has remained virtually untouched all this time in the laboratory, apart from logging, that is writing down the key or edge numbers of each scene and breaking down the separate scenes in much the same way as was done in the cutting room with the rushes. But with one major difference, that all handling has to be done wearing cotton gloves and in spotless and dust-free conditions.

When the cutting copy is received at the lab, a negative cutter is allocated to the film whose job is to match the negative scene by scene to the cutting copy, cutting the negative to the right length. This is done by putting the cutting copy into a synchroniser and running the negative in synch with the print, having matched exactly the key numbers. Each piece of negative is then joined to the next by a special joiner which uses a kind of hot welding process.

When the negative is loaded into the printer, to avoid the possibility of the joins jumping, especially in the case of 16mm negative, a system may be used called A & B rolls. Here the cut negative is assembled in two rolls and the length of the negative on the A roll extended slightly beyond the cut indicated in the cutting copy. The incoming scene is similarly extended on the B roll and the exact position of the cut made by an automatic device on the printer. In order to keep the two rolls of negative in synch, black film or spacing is used.

When the picture negative of each reel has been cut, the start has to be synchronised with the respective start marks on both picture and sound optical negatives and academy leaders joined front and end. Academy leaders are the standard leaders with start marks and numbers at one foot intervals which assist the projectionist in lacing up the projector. Their name derives from the standard format drawn up by the Academy of Motion Picture Arts and Sciences in Hollywood.

## Grading and printing

Upon completion of the negative cutting, the film now passes to the colour grader for his assessment of each scene for colour printing. He may have notes provided by the editor, director or cameraman advising him of any special treatment required in any scene, night shots for example.

The film is now ready for a first colour combined (that is picture and sound on one piece of film) optical print to be made. This may be called an answer, **grading** or merely first print and at this stage, it is useful if the cameraman can see it with the grader. Very often by this time he is away on another film and so it is up to the producer, director and editor to make their comments with the grader's own, for it is fairly rare for the first print to be perfect in every respect.

And so further prints are made (their number may be restricted if the budget is stretched by now) until all grading adjustments have been made and a show copy is produced which, as its name suggests, is suitable for public showing.

In order to protect the precious original negative, a copy negative (CRI – colour reversal internegative) is also made and prints from this may require further grading adjustments. It is from these CRIs that the bulk prints for release to cinemas are made.

## The final stages

And so the production processes of a feature film are complete apart from various tidying up affairs such as preparation of release scripts, a complete list of each shot with timings, picture and sound (see Figure 16 page 59), preparation of trailers,

| Scene No. Foot. | Action/Dialogue | Spot No. | Start | End | Total |
|---|---|---|---|---|---|
| Sc.74 Cont: | WILSON TURNS, LOOKS R. | | | | |
| 75 Starts 746.03 | M. WAIST SHOT MAN L, DEVRIL R. WILSON (O.S.):   God help him, who was it? | 1/11 | 746.05 | 748.05 | 2.00 |
| 76 Starts 748.11 | C.U. BUSHES - TIGER ENTERS R IN M.S. - PAN L AND TILT UP AS HE RUNS INTO B.G.   TIGER: GROWLS | | | | |
| 77 Starts 750.13 | M. WAIST SHOT WILSON - LOOKS R. WILSON:   Bloody fool. | 1/12 | 751.04 | 753.06 | 2.02 |
| 78 Starts 753.09 | NATIVES ENTER L AND R IN M.L.S. (BACK TO CAMERA) CROWD AROUND PIECE OF BONE LYING ON FLOOR. | | | | |
| 79 Starts 757.07 | UP TO M. WAIST SHOT WILSON LOOKS F.G. L. WILSON TO   (INDIAN) BEATERS: | 1/13 | 757.11 | 759.06 | 1.11 |
| 80 Starts 759.14 | M.L.S. NATIVES - WILLIAM ENTERS F.G. R IN M. WAIST SHOT (BACK TO CAMERA) - RUNS TO B.G. NATIVES.   FX: CHATTER   WILLIAM (BACK TO CAMERA) TO NATIVES):   Get back, get back ...   WILLIAM KNEELS.   TIGER (O.S.): GROWLS | 1/14 | 762.01 | 764.05 | 2.04 |
| 81 Starts 769.13 | (HIGH ANGLE) DOWN TO M.L.S. PIECE OF BONE LYING ON GROUND - TILT UP AS WILLIAM EXAMINES BONE.   WILLIAM TO   Plenty of blood -- WILSON:   and a bit of bone. | 1/15 | 777.07 | 781.06 | 3.15 |

Fig. 16. Release script.

registration and censorship, completion of the accounts and arrangements for publicity and marketing.

## GETTING INTO FEATURE FILM MAKING

## Scriptwriter

Obviously, the first requirement is to have the desire, ability and talent to write and, in the case of features, to appreciate what will make a good film story for cinema audiences.

Feature scriptwriters often share their time or move from writing for the theatre, books, television, journalism, advertising or documentary film making.

There are various ways of studying to be a scriptwriter:

1.  By acquiring existing scripts, many of which are published in book form from specialist bookshops like Zwemmers, 80 Charing Cross Road, London WC2 or The Cinema Bookshop, 13/14 Great Russell Street, London WC1B 3NH.

2.  By reading the wealth of 'how to' books on scriptwriting (such as Screenwriting for the 21st Century) available from specialist bookshops listed in the British Film Institute Film and Television Handbook (see Appendix).

3.  By trying to get employment as a **reader** for a film or television production company. Readers assess the potential of the masses of ideas submitted and provide a chance for you to see the good and the bad and study those that eventually make it to the screen.

4.  By taking a course at a reputable film school where professional scriptwriters visit or are employed as lecturers (see Chapter 7 on Training).

5. By attending courses run by TAPS. Contact them at Shepperton Studios, Shepperton, Middx TW17 0QD. Tel: (01932) 591151. Website: *www.tapsnet.org*

Assuming you have already written a treatment or outline script, send a copy to suitable literary agents, directors, producers and/or production companies and enclose a stamped addressed envelope if you want it returned. Keep a note of where you send copies and if there is a glimmer of response from anywhere, telephone to arrange a meeting. Even if comments are negative, seek advice and suggestions as to other people who might be interested.

## Production Department

These are the typical jobs in a Production Department:

Production manager
Assistant director (first, second or third)
Production supervisor (or production secretary)
Script supervisor (or Continuity)
Production accountant
Bookkeeper
Secretarial
Runner/tea person

All these jobs are organisational and administrative to a greater or lesser degree. They are not necessarily short cuts to creative jobs although there have, of course, been exceptions, especially with runners. Even though this job might be considered by some to be humble and very often it can entail long hours and hectic patches with minimum reward, it gives someone with ambition the chance to study the organisational side of production and, more importantly, to get to know a wide range of people.

For any of the jobs in this department with the possible exception of assistant directors, office and secretarial skills are almost essential. Certainly being able to type and being computer literate is always useful, especially at times of stress when secretarial services may not be available.

The accounts department obviously requires the same qualifications that are called for in any business and the specialised knowledge of film production relating to accountancy is usually acquired on the job.

Someone with bookkeeping or accountancy experience who subsequently attends a film school would be at a distinct advantage when it came to getting employment and several producers have come from the ranks of accountants.

Anyone keen to be involved in any of the jobs on the organisational side of features should write to the production manager of feature film companies, stressing any organisational experience and office skills such as typing or word processing. Any involvement or special interest in films such as secretary of a film society, school film club or drama group would attract attention.

Parallel experience in other media like radio, television or advertising might give the edge to your application and, as with all job seeking, try to get an interview and seek advice and suggestions of other people to whom you might write.

Remember that, unless you are applying for a known vacancy, the chance of your letter arriving at the precise moment that a feature film is being set up and a production unit put together is pretty slim.

The bulk of jobs in features are freelance and the nature of freelance work, even for the most experienced, is keeping your ear to the ground so that you are up to date with what films are being planned and the projected start dates. Studying news in the trade papers (see Appendix) is useful although not always reliable! There are several websites with job vacancies too. Try *www.mandy.com* or *www.shootingpeople.com*

## Art department

Designer
Art director
Draughtsman
Set dresser
Property buyer
Runner

This is a department where in the case of the first three jobs, training outside the industry is a virtual necessity. As well as having the ability to draw, this could be skill in technical drawing, architecture or, in the case of titles or signwriting, graphic design.

Set dressers and property buyers should be able to read and interpret plans and have the ability to find relevant items called for by the designer, especially in films with other than a contemporary setting.

Once again, as in all job seeking, it is a question of research finding out what productions are being set up by which companies. Write to the production manager or the designer or art director working on a particular project in its early stages and state your qualifications and offer to bring examples of your work. Stress your interest in the design of feature films, and any research you may have done into the subject of set design in past films.

An advantage of working in the art department is that due to the sporadic nature of feature film production, periods of inactivity between films can be filled with work in parallel fields such as architecture, exhibition work or theatre.

## Costume design

Costume designer
Wardrobe
Runner

Formal art school or practical training in the garment industry is really necessary. Many costume designers started in the theatre and indeed may share their time continuing to do theatre work between films so theatre experience is useful for a newcomer too.

Working in collaboration with the designer and the lighting cameraman is part of the job and therefore colour co-ordination and knowledge of materials, both from a practical and budgetary point of view, is necessary.

The costume designer's work may overflow at times of panic into the practicalities of dressmaking and fitting and although wardrobe is basically responsible for ensuring the right clothes are there in the right condition, impeccably pressed or suitably dirtied down, at the right time and place, this job may also overflow into on the spot adaptation or repairs. So practical skills are required plus the ability to adapt to working conditions which, on location, are not always ideal.

For jobs in this area, write to the production manager or the costume designer and besides giving your qualifications and practical experience, stress your appreciation of the fact that you have to be adaptable to unexpected situations and squeezed schedules.

## Casting director or artists' agent

People who do these jobs may have moved from being actors themselves, as extensive knowledge of the profession is required and, in the case of casting director, knowledge of agents and their clients. Additionally, good organisation and negotiating skills are required and many people have acquired these through secretarial experience in production offices or by working in agents' offices.

Knowledge of contemporary film, television and theatre with regard to casting and contact with drama schools are additional attributes plus the ability to read a script and match suitable, available and affordable artists to the characters, although, apart from the very smallest parts, the director normally has the final say.

If you want to start in this department and are not already established as an actor, the best way in is via office jobs but when you apply, try to convince people of your knowledge of the current casts of films, stage productions and television dramas.

## Camera department

Lighting cameraman
Camera operator
Focus puller
Clapper/loader
Grip
VT operator
Runner

Traditionally in feature films the route into this department has been via clapper/loader and progression through focus puller to camera operator and thence to lighting cameraman.

However, experience in other fields such as documentary or television and qualifications from a reputable film school have led to people becoming lighting cameramen much quicker on features now.

Experience and interest in still photography as an amateur or professional is always a good foundation for entry to the camera department and with the growth of cheaper video cameras, there is no reason why aspiring entrants cannot produce examples of their work, however ham-fisted.

But this is an area of the industry where a variety of training opportunities exist and so unless you are convinced that 'on job' training is the only route for you, formal training courses are preferable, if only because you get the opportunity for hands-on experience in all jobs using a variety of equipment.

'On job' knowledge can be obtained by applying to companies that hire out equipment and services to features and this would probably be one of the best points of entry for grips. But the work consists largely of checking and maintaining equipment and you would therefore have to convince the company of your ability to handle sophisticated mechanical things and your knowledge of lenses.

For lists of facilities companies, consult the trade directories listed in the Appendix. If applying for work in the camera department of a particular feature film, write to the production manager or the lighting cameraman, who is normally responsible for engaging his own camera crew.

## Editing department

Editor
Dubbing editor
Assistant editor (first, second or third)

Undoubtedly one of the best starting points for any branch of film production – features, documentaries, commercials and so on – is via the cutting room, or editing suite.

Here is a chance to examine the work of other people in design, camera, sound, direction, even budgets and how wisely or otherwise money has been spent. All of which means that anyone with ultimate ambitions to direct or produce could not do better than consider the cutting room as a possible initial stepping stone.

That is not to say that the job of editor is not wholly satisfying in itself and many editors have temperaments better suited to working in the confines of the cutting room and thus contributing their talents to the effectiveness of the film.

The normal progression in the case of features is from third to second to first assistant editor and thence the chance to edit. Between features, many editors and cutting room staff may fill in with work on documentaries or commercials with their shorter schedules and it is here that the experienced assistant editor may stand a better chance of being able to do some actual editing.

Write to the editor of any feature film set up or to the production manager if the editor has not been appointed. Experience in handling film is still possible through membership of a film society making amateur movies, working in a film laboratory (see page 54) or working for a company supplying numbering services (see page 42).

Apart from training at a film school or **FT2** (see page 156), the more usual route into feature cutting rooms is via experience in documentaries, commercials or television.

There are companies that provide editing facilities for a variety of productions but it is rare for these companies to be asked to take on a feature film. (See Chapters 3 and 4 dealing with Commercials and Documentaries.)

Bigger budget feature films may employ runners in the cutting room and this time honoured starting point is as ideal here as in any department. But a word of warning about the job of runner anywhere. Don't think it'll be a soft option – it can be extremely hard work with long hours and don't look at it necessarily as leading to promotion five minutes after you've started the job.

Be patient, do the job well and use the time to make contacts and learn from observing other people at work.

## Director

The commonest illusion among people who nurse an ambition to 'get into films or television' is that they all want to direct. This is often due to ignorance of the structure of the industry and of the great number of jobs that may be available in other departments in all the different areas of film and programme making.

A few years ago, David Puttnam addressing a gathering of several hundred film students began with these remarks: 'It is possible that three or four of you here today may succeed in becoming film directors'. After the ensuing shattered silence, he then developed his theme of the few opportunities that realistically exist for directors compared to the number with aspirations.

This is not to decry ambition but merely to present a practical approach to becoming a director; for equally certainly, in spite of recurrent crises in feature film production, there is a constant need to encourage new talent, especially now that the dividing line becomes more blurred between films for cinemas with subsequent release on video or DVD, films financed or made especially for television and television financed films made for release in cinemas prior to TV release.

So how do you set about becoming a feature film director? Undoubtedly the best chances come to students who have completed a course at one of the leading film schools (see Chapter 7 Training) and who have made an impressive graduation film; and from a budgetary point of view and from demonstrating talent and imagination in the use of film technique, the shorter the better. A short film, say 10-15 minutes long, is preferable from another more mundane standpoint. Film producers and production executives lead very busy and stressful existences and their time is overflowing with a mass of meetings, punctuated by telephone interruptions and visitors who, in their mind, may be more important than a newcomer's presentation. A short film should display the potential of its director right from the start and there is therefore a better chance that the viewer might remain hooked without interruption.

But no producer is likely to engage a director for a feature film on the strength of one short. So what are the other ingredients to bolster your presentation?

An option or the rights in a property that will make a good feature film – a book, play, treatment or script – could certainly be attractive. And if the aspiring director also has access to finance, this could appeal to a producer as well!

But the fact is that very few outsiders stand any chance of becoming a feature film director without having acquired experience in other fields such as feature film editing, directing commercials, documentaries, television drama or directing in the theatre.

So the most sensible advice for those whose ultimate ambition is to direct feature films is to enrol at an accredited film school and/or gain a foundation of experience as outlined above.

## Producer

From the beginning of the film industry there have always been producer/directors who have wanted to control every aspect of a film. Chaplin is probably the best example of these showmen/impresarios.

But the size and complexity of the financial and organisational side of feature film production means that most directors now prefer to leave this part of the operation to a producer so as to allow them to concentrate more on the creative elements.

The producer's more detached view should however be of value to the director when it comes to constructive criticism of the film's effectiveness, especially if the producer has worked his way up through production. The relationship between producer and director may be a delicate one but, with mutual respect, can be extremely rewarding to both.

So, assuming your ultimate aim is to be 'captain of the ship', with a preference for organisational and entrepreneurial skills and with only the lightest touch to the creative tiller, what are the best starting points and possible routes to the top?

It would be a very exceptional person who could find and acquire the rights to a subject, interest a director and assemble the necessary finance to set up as a producer from scratch but it could be done without any previous experience whatsoever.

But to be realistic, the more likely progression, as with directors, is via formal training at a film school and experience in other technical and/or administrative areas of feature films or, most likely of all, via experience in other branches of film making such as documentaries, commercials or television leading to producing more modest projects than a feature film.

Experience in accountancy or business studies are both helpful assets as are general organisational and leadership skills. The setting up, mounting, production and completion of a feature film is a major commercial enterprise when it is considered that the producer is responsible for a budget that may run into many millions of dollars. The final product will be expected to appeal to a wide international market and have a long life with a variety of outlets. So the final attribute of a producer is to have that indefinable entrepreneurial vision, with an instinct for what the public wants. And that is a rare talent indeed!

So if you think that you can take on the frustrations, responsibilities and possible rewards of being a producer, then the most practical advice is precisely the same as suggested in the last paragraph devoted to directors above: enrol for training at an accredited film school, followed by the broadest experience possible in other departments of feature films or other areas of film making.

In parallel, you should always be keeping a lookout for suitable subjects to acquire and develop in collaboration with a writer and director. And always foster any contacts with access to finance. And if you haven't a clue where to go for funding, there is a website, *www.shootingpeople.org* which will guide you to their book *UK Film Finance Guide*.

## Craft grades
Carpenter
Plasterer

Painter

Rigger

Electrician

Make-up

Hairdresser

Wardrobe

Props

Upholsterer/drapes

Construction manager

Plumber

Scaffolder

All the above crafts, excluding electrician, have traditionally in feature films come under the umbrella of BECTU – The Broadcasting Entertainment Cinematograph and Theatre Union, as do other specialised, though not in the film sense, technical jobs such as driver, nurse or catering staff.

Although changes in legislation regarding trade unions mean that the closed shop can no longer exist, the union in this case continues to exert influence and safeguard the rates of pay and conditions of its members in feature films.

Specific craft training geared only to feature films, apart from that operated by FT2 (see page 156) is still fairly sparse. General training and qualifications from colleges, or 'on job' training outside the film industry for the particular skill that interests you most, is the best foundation on which you can base your entry into features. Thereafter there are limited possible vacancies for apprentices and trainees in all grades.

Skillset, the UK Film Council and the union are concerned at the lack of formal training which they maintain with justification will lead to skill shortages in the future. It is therefore advisable for anyone wanting to work in any of the crafts listed above to consult BECTU whose address is: 373–377 Clapham Road, London SW9 9BT. Tel: (020) 7346 0900 or SKILLSET (see page 147).

Electricians need a minimum four years' apprenticeship and appropriate City and Guilds Qualification. Contact: Unite the Union, 33–37 Morland Street, London EC1V 8HA. Tel: (020) 7780 4107.

See also Chapter 7 on Training for electricians and other crafts.

## Projection

Studios, apart from the very smallest and those that operate entirely as 'four wallers', usually have their own viewing theatres for screening rushes and for the use of the cutting rooms.

The projectors are similar in many respects to those in commercial cinemas and are operated by projectionists. Projectionists operate the projectors in recording and dubbing theatres as well.

The job of a projectionist on the production side of feature films is very similar to that of a projectionist in a commercial cinema with the exception that in production the projectionist may be operating for shorter periods of frantic activity, lacing up and showing shorter lengths of film, re-showing them immediately and collaborating with other technicians such as editors and cameramen who expect the utmost quality as they may be checking some suspected fault such as focus or steadiness.

This means that maintenance of equipment features high on the work schedule of studio and production projectionists and speed and adaptability are other useful skills.

Experience in the basic mechanics of projectors and the handling of 35mm film can be gained by working in a commercial cinema and there are many eminent people in the film industry who started their careers in this way.

As in the case of working in the cutting room, the projectionist sees a film in its raw state and often makes contact with other technicians from directors and editors at the rushes stage to dubbing editors and recordists if working in post production recording theatres. Knowledge of laboratory work can often be acquired, for example colour and sound quality; and this, in turn, can lead to interests in film stocks, lenses and cameras.

And so the job of projectionist, important though it is as part of the whole production process, is also useful as a route to other departments.

The way in to the job is via the studios who rent out their facilities including theatres to feature film producers. Other companies may offer only viewing, dubbing and recording facilities, not only to features but to other areas of film making.

The names of these companies and of the studios can be found in the directories listed in the Appendix.

Write to the studio manager of studios or the managing director of companies stating your experience in a commercial cinema or even in handling 16mm projectors for a film society, at school or in the church hall and stress your commitment to film and to showing it in the best possible conditions, backed up by your interest in the latest projection equipment.

## Publicity

Publicists, whether employed exclusively on a feature film and hence called unit publicists, or working for a company that is responsible for publicity on a number of projects, invariably move from being journalists or from working in public relations.

Stills photographers may be employed in the same way and also tend to come from newspapers and magazines.

The job of a unit stills photographer, besides requiring technical skills and, as in newspapers, the ability to work fast in a variety of conditions, has what can sometimes be an additionally difficult aspect. Stills are required for publicity purposes of virtually every key scene of a film and are usually done after a satisfactory take. The order from the assistant director to 'hold it for a still' may be recognised by everybody as a necessity but on top of sometimes pent up emotions following a particularly difficult scene, the stills photographer is not always welcome, hence the need for speed and tact.

Tact is also an asset for publicists, coping with the moods and whims of stars or temperamental directors. But, besides this, the ability to write is the first requirement.

There can be opportunities in the publicity department of a feature film or a publicity company for runners or office juniors but if you confess any ambition to progress when you are interviewed for these jobs, the minimum requirement would be A level English. An English degree and a proven ability to write might also help your promotion.

Write to the unit publicist of a feature film in preparation or, if one has not been appointed, to the production manager. In the case of companies specialising in publicity, write to the managing director (see Appendix for listings).

## Sound department

Sound recordist
Boom operator or boom swinger
Sound mixer
Sound assistant

On feature films the minimum sound crew originally stipulated by the union for shooting 'on the floor', that is in a studio or on location, used to be three: a recordist, boom swinger and maintenance person.

The equipment was bulkier and less reliable and holdups due to technical faults were costly and frustrating. Now that recording gear is simpler and lighter, the normal crew is two, replacement of faulty equipment being easier than carrying out maintenance on the spot.

Of course, knowledge of the equipment is necessary for anyone in the sound department, and some theory of recording techniques is as well, but, almost as important, both for floor recordists and sound mixers in recording and dubbing theatres, is a familiarity and 'feel' both for the equipment and the quality of the sound.

This applies equally to the boom swinger who must have the same 'feel' and memory for dialogue as spoken by the various artists so as to be able to anticipate the best position for the microphone(s) during recording. A knowledge of camera lenses is also necessary to avoid the intrusion of the microphone into the picture area during a shot.

Sound recording certainly forms part of any film school training and there are other specialised short courses (see Chapter 7 on Training) but experience for those keen to work in features can be obtained, as in other departments, by working on more modest productions such as documentaries.

Apart from FT2 (see page 156), there are very few opportunities for the inexperienced person to get into feature film making on the production sound crew. In recording or dubbing theatres, however, there may be vacancies for runners and/or tea persons and this can lead to becoming a sound assistant who supervises and loads with tape the equipment that actually does the recording. Besides knowledge and dexterity in the use of the machines, this job also requires an orderly mind as tape has to be filed and accounted for and records and report sheets filled in.

Continuing experience here can certainly lead to becoming either a recordist or mixer. Although in the case of the latter there can be considerable creative input, floor and studio recordists have fewer creative opportunities but their jobs certainly demand high degrees of skill and technical knowledge.

The potential newcomer to a department as competitive as any other in features is well advised to accumulate as much technical qualification as possible, backed up by experience in other areas of film making or sound recording which might include radio or music. There are plenty of opportunities too to acquire experience in sound recording as an amateur.

Write to the production manager or the sound recordist if you think you have sufficient qualifications and/or experience for floor recording jobs or the head of sound or managing director of a recording or dubbing theatre, either attached to a studio or set up as a separate company to provide these facilities for feature films (see Appendix for directories).

## Laboratory work

Negative cutter
Colour grader
Optical printer
Laboratory contact

In former days a 'catch 22' situation existed in the film industry whereby it was not possible to get a job without being a member of a trade union and membership was impossible without first having a job. Working in a film laboratory where vacancies sometimes occurred, especially in the more routine developing and printing areas, was a popular way of obtaining the much sought after union ticket with the aim of transferring to another part of the film industry at some later date.

Laboratory work is still a vital part of the whole production process although now severely restricted. But for those with scientific leanings it may be every bit as satisfying as the more creative areas of production. In addition, the jobs listed above involve considerable liaison with cameramen and editors for example. Stanley Kubrick, the feature film producer who died in 1999, still insisted on seeing every single print of any film he produced in the presence of the laboratory people concerned.

The starting points are therefore in developing, printing and cleaning for which no formal qualifications are necessarily required beyond GCSE but an interest in photography as an amateur is an advantage.

Write to the managing director or personnel department of laboratories (see Appendix for directories).

The approach of DVD (Digital Video Disc) for recording the original material and screening the finished production on DVD will revolutionize showings in cinemas, but this development is still some way off.

## SUMMING UP

Jobs in feature film production are almost entirely freelance and have always been oversubscribed at every level. They depend on keeping up to date (through the trade magazines, for example) with what productions are being planned and being virtually on the spot at the crucial moment when starting dates are fixed and crews being signed up.

There are three publications devoted solely to supplying this information. *PCR (Production and casting report)* and *FILMLOG* (£29 for five weeks and £133 for 26 weeks) are available on subscription only. They are not cheap but it is money well spent for the determined. Particulars from: P O Box 100, Broadstairs, Kent CT10 1UJ. Tel: (01843) 860885 or (01715) 668282.

The third is: *Advance Production News*, Crimson Communications, 211A Station House, 49 Greenwich High Road, London SE10 8JL. Tel: (020) 8293 5015. Website: *www.crimsonuk.com*

There are two good websites for all sorts of jobs (not just features) at *www.shootingpeople.org* and *www.mandy.com*

Jobs in other areas of production made on film is useful experience to proffer when applying for work in features and, because they are likely to last for shorter periods, still allow you to look for jobs in features in parallel.

There are so many elements of film and television production in, for example, commercials, pop videos or documentaries that are similar to features that the next chapters will not go into nearly as much detail and it is therefore suggested that the reader refers back frequently to this first chapter.

# 3

# Commercials

## COMMERCIALS AS MINI-FEATURES

Commercials, whether for showing in cinemas or on television, are still often made on 35mm film and therefore, from a production point of view, may be looked at as mini-features.

The romantic entanglements of Nicole and Papa with their Renault Clios are good examples.

But with running times of anything from 10 seconds to 2 minutes (20, 30 and 40 seconds being the commonest lengths), the cost per foot of finished film may often exceed that of a feature film.

It is only in the final editing that the introduction of computer-generated special effects, computerised animation and graphics may differ from the completion process of feature films, although features use these techniques as well.

It is now possible to transfer video to 35mm film but unless the video is High Definition (1,000 lines or more resolution), the quality is not great. But the introduction of Digital Non-linear systems of editing has meant that the transfer of film to disc and back again is perfectly satisfactory. (See Chapter 4, Documentaries, page 92.) And soon, shooting, editing and screening or transmitting on DVD (Digital Video Disc) may become the norm.

Of course, all the effects that can be achieved digitally can still be done by conventional animation techniques or optically in a laboratory but the time and cost involved before results can be seen usually conflicts with the inevitably squeezed production and delivery schedules imposed by the advertising agencies.

## ADVERTISING AGENCIES

It is in the agencies that commercials are born. And it is to the agencies that commercials production companies look for their livelihoods. The agencies invariably write the scripts, commission the whole production and, having supplied 100% of the finance, therefore own the copyright and the actual film and video material.

The agencies are acting on behalf of their clients whose products or services they have been commissioned to advertise, and the use of commercials may be only part of an overall campaign employing other media like press, posters or radio and the theme running through all the advertising may be linked.

There may be common factors in the casting of actors, the design and style of the production and this involves close liaison between the agency, their client and the production company.

Even though the total running time is short, the production cost is so high and the money spent on air time on television even higher that every second on the screen has to be analysed and made as effective as possible. This is why the script has to be vetted by everybody concerned with the campaign.

## Storyboards and animatics

To help visualise the script, artists may also prepare **storyboards** (see page 85) and the agency may also prepare a trial commercial (sometimes called an **animatic**), filming the storyboard and adding a sound track to reassure everybody that the ideas really work.

This is not to say that when a really talented director receives a script, helps with a storyboard or sees a trial commercial, he cannot add an enormous amount of extra flair and individuality. In fact it could be said that in recent years there has been more creative innovation in the making of commercials and pop videos than in any other area of production.

So if you think you have the talent for writing scripts for commercials, try for a job in an agency with a busy film and television department; there is no better route to working later in a production company.

Similarly, agency producers in these departments, although not quite carrying out the role of a producer on, say, a feature film, get to understand the business of production so well that they are often tempted to set up their own production company and either take on directing or producing commercials themselves or hire directors.

## COMMERCIALS PRODUCTION

Commercials production companies are often fairly small set-ups built around the talents of one or more directors. Several of

Fig. 17. Storyboard for a commercial.

them may however be controlled financially by one group. Sometimes they may have an option on the services of a top feature director who is usually happy to direct commercials between making feature films.

The actual preparation, setting up, scheduling and shooting of a commercial is virtually the same as for a feature film except that the overall schedule is more likely to be measured in days rather than months.

There is another major difference. In the case of features, the whole organisation to make the film will probably have started from nothing; in the case of a commercials production company which depends on continuity of work, the basic company structure is permanent. This will include one or more producers and directors, a production manager, accountants, secretaries and runners in smart offices accessible to the advertising agencies. Some companies have their own editing facilities but many use outside facilities companies, depending on the amount and style of the editing required.

Thus, as with feature films, the design, camera, sound and the rest of the production department like assistant directors, script supervisors and so on will be engaged on a freelance basis for a single or series of commercials. So the same advice applies to anyone wanting to get into feature films (see Chapter 2 on Features).

There are some basic differences.

■  First, because companies who specialise in commercials have a permanent basic set-up, they are more easily contacted through directories listed in the Appendix.

■ Secondly, there is more likelihood of employment for runners, tea persons, gofers, receptionists, secretaries or bookkeepers as the volume of production may increase at very short notice.

The success of commercials production companies depends very much on the talent and popularity in the advertising agencies of individual directors and these may even be a matter of fashion. So the amount of work can go down equally dramatically.

## THE WAY IN TO COMMERCIALS

One way to discover the most active agencies and the most favoured production companies is to study the trade papers like *Campaign, Broadcast, Marketing Week* or *Marketing* and then write to the agencies and/or production companies that feature most strongly.

In addition to the job opportunities similar to feature films and the possibility of administrative jobs in production companies, let us examine the post-production of commercials and the various jobs involved.

## POST-PRODUCTION

The editing of commercials follows virtually the same procedure as for features but, as stated in the note on page 38, editing on film has been increasingly superseded by digital non-linear editing. So what happens using this system and how does it affect possible starting points for people wanting to get into post-production?

Assuming the production has been shot on film, the exposed negative is sent to the laboratory as usual for processing but instead of a print being made, all the material is transferred to videotape which is sent to the editor as soon as possible. The assistant editor will then digitise the footage on to a computer desk-top editing system. The editor can now start assembling and rough editing the production. Pressures sometimes mean that this has to be done at night when the edit suite is available. The big advantage of this system is that the editor can get instant access to all video and audio material.

So, as with film, editing proceeds to a fine cut and, when everyone is satisfied (and with commercials this includes the client), the material is passed to a dubbing editor for all the sound tracks (music, sound effects and dialogue) to be edited in at the right places but still all on disk, the sound having been transferred from whatever the original was recorded on. After the dubbing editor has laid down all the sound into a sound station, the whole thing passes to a dubbing mixer for all the tracks to be mixed at the right levels but instead of doing this in a dubbing theatre (see page 54) the mixing is done on to a further disk via computer. Only when this has been completed can the disk be transferred to digital tape and thence to an optical sound negative which is developed in the laboratory, and the film is then ready for combined printing if it is to be shown in cinemas (see page 58).

For television programmes, commercials and features similar routes apply and certainly require the same skills and talent from the editors, but they must have the additional ability to operate computers. There are assistants employed at every stage and, here again, computer literacy or the ability to learn quickly is absolutely essential.

## STARTING POINTS IN POST-PRODUCTION

### Editing

Some production companies have their own editing facilities but many use companies that provide an editing service to different companies. These may have clients who produce commercials, documentaries or television programmes.

Their success depends on the reputation of the editors and their relationships with directors and their facilities but they also employ assistant editors and administrative staff such as receptionists and runners. So one good starting point is via these companies who can be found in the various directories listed in the Appendix.

### Recording

A few production companies may have their own recording theatres for voice overs and dubbing but most use outside facilities.

As with editing services these recording companies have clients in different areas of production and in addition to recordists or recording engineers have recording assistants and administrative personnel including the ubiquitous runners.

So if your ambitions lie in the recording field and particularly in the invariably tight schedules of commercials production, go for vacancies in these companies.

Knowledge and qualifications in sound (see Chapter 7 on Training) obviously may be an advantage in the case of recording assistants, but enthusiasm and willingness to learn on the job or by attending courses once employed are almost as important if you're starting as a runner or a receptionist.

## Post-production facilities

Post-production facility companies have both editing and sound equipment and also provide visual effects so they are really a 'one-stop shop'.

However, the ever increasing complexity of digital editing and its parallel facilities of graphics and effects means that technical training in these areas is definitely advisable (see Chapter 7 on Training) before looking for a job with these companies.

## SUMMING UP

Working in commercials is a hectic existence but, provided you accept that the advertising agency is finally the king, it can be creatively satisfying, the money is good and it can be a stepping stone to other areas of production. The techniques used are often in the vanguard of creative inventiveness, mixing film and video, live action narrative, abstract animation, manipulated images, all edited on the latest non-linear editing system.

So if you are keen to work in commercials, study the technical press (see page 87) to find out the advertising agencies, production companies and directors who are most active and approach them via the directories (see Appendix).

## NEW MEDIA

This is a growing area of production which encompasses the Internet, Intranet (internal communications via computer links) and DVD authoring for corporate and commercial use.

All these, as far as jobs are concerned, are really variations on commercials, documentary, animation and print production with producers, programmers, technical developers, managers and designers. There may be the usual openings for newcomers taking the tea person/runner route but with one essential difference. Any hope of advancement must include computer literacy and IT skills, and keeping abreast of rapidly changing technical and creative developments.

For information about companies operating in this area, consult the trade magazines like *Televisual* and *New Media Age*.

# 4

# Documentaries

John Grierson, acknowledged to be the inventor of the word, defined 'documentary' as an attempt to build up with a camera a true but nevertheless dramatised version of life. This means that just as in any other film or video presentation, apart from live coverage of events, a good script is the key to success.

Screenings of documentaries fall mainly into two separate areas

- theatrical
- non-theatrical

By theatrical is meant showings in cinemas (a comparative rarity), on television or by the sale or rental of videocassettes or similar means like DVD.

By non-theatrical is meant showings to non-paying audiences, either specially invited or through free or nominal rental or sale, usually via film or DVD libraries to schools, universities or any specialist organisations in industry, medicine or other professional or social groups. In this category can also be included Business Television Networks which are usually transmitted via satellite to employees or potential customers. In the UK there are at least 56 such networks, in Europe 29 and in the USA 310, all of which add up to over 50,000 hours of programming a year. Some of these corporate projects may have bigger budgets and better production values than some television programmes.

## PRODUCTION

The production of documentaries is now almost exclusively on video. But if it is intended at the outset that major showings will be for audiences of 200 or more on as large a screen as possible, then film is still preferable, with subsequent showings transferred to video for smaller audiences which may be down to one person running a program on DVD on their computer. Equally, there are some situations in remote or rugged locations where film cameras may be more adaptable and reliable, being mechanical rather than electronic.

Conversely, the ever increasing sophistication, simplification and portability of video equipment means that productions whose release are predominantly on a TV screen originate more and more on video, with, in the case of Business Television, a percentage of live transmission interspersed with pre-recorded film or video sequences.

Unfortunately, although the technology exists for recording in extra high quality video for high definition television (HDTV) enabling the projection of pictures on to screens as large and with quality as good as film projection, the equipment is not yet universally available at anything like realistic costs. Nevertheless, original recording on HDTV or even disc with subsequent transfer to film, projection on disc or anything else is becoming more feasible.

## DOCUMENTARY SUBJECTS

The major 'theatrical' subjects for documentaries are:

- travel
- adventure
- wildlife
- science
- art
- sport
- current affairs and history
- social problems
- home improvements
- reality TV

Not so well known perhaps is the enormous range of subjects in the **non-theatrical** field, some of which overlap with the above:

- teaching and instructional
- sales (either direct or indirect)
- propaganda (however cunningly disguised)
- recruitment
- public relations
- health and safety

## SPONSORSHIP

There is one major difference in the two sectors and that is that invariably films made for non-theatrical audiences have been sponsored by whoever is interested in putting over their message to a particular audience. This may be so broad that they would like to reach as wide and large an audience as possible and therefore are delighted if they succeed in getting a television showing for the production they have sponsored, in cash or kind. Travel documentaries sponsored by airlines or tourist offices are good examples.

In many countries there is still an aversion to showing sponsored programmes, however obliquely slanted and brilliantly carried out. But with the increasing cost of production, this is an area that may well see more changes just as sports sponsorship has come to be accepted virtually everywhere.

## JOB DIFFERENCES IN DOCUMENTARIES

So what are the differences and additional entry points for someone keen on the production of documentaries?

### Scripts

First the script, which is more akin to journalism but thinking in primarily visual terms. Thus a good article on a technical subject with long quotes from experts may be absolutely non-visual apart from long sequences of 'talking heads', a type of presentation all too common on television but by no means the most exciting way of putting a subject across.

This visual imagination and good construction of the script with a strong opening, a logical development, periodic punctuation points and an exciting climax, applies equally to the documentary aimed at the widest international audience as to the most specialised subject, for example medical, aimed at highly specialised viewers.

So the first task for the potential documentary scriptwriter is to narrow down the broad subject areas that interest you most. Of course, experienced writers maintain that, like journalists, any subject can be researched sufficiently deeply for a presentation that may run for a comparatively short time. But it would be foolish for the most part to put yourself forward for example for

SEQUENCE 1.          We begin in black and white.  A cluster of wooden
(Pre-title)          drilling rigs litter the side of a steep hill.  The
                     grass has been ripped away, exposing earth and rock
                     outcropping.  Interspersed among the rigs are shacks:
                     smoke is coming from a chimney towards the centre of
                     the cluster.  In the foreground is a small field
                     office, that will double for the Malamute Saloon after
                     work.  On the office steps a group of thickset men turn
                     and studiedly challenge the camera.  It is Oil Creek,
                     Pennsylvania, 1865.

                     The scene continues as the narrator states that the
                     nature of each industry is described by the language
                     that it uses.  Words are trapped by years.  "Christmas
                     tree", "rough neck" and "wild cat" are pioneer words,
                     visual and virile.  They represent the bravery,
                     enterprise and muscle that were the qualities of those
                     early pioneers.  But terms such as 'interface',
                     'process' and 'systems' reveal the modern
                     professionalism of the offshore oil and gas industry.
                     They are thought and skill words, implying different
                     codes of conduct and practice.

                     DISSOLVE TO:

SEQUENCE 2.          A three dimensional computer graphic of the interior
                     network of a reservoir.  We move more through the
                     matrix along the pathways and tunnels.  The narrator
                     continues, saying that these new terms point to a quite
                     different attitude towards the reservoir.  The pioneer's
                     rush for the bonanza has given way to the
                     professional's meticulously rational approach.  The
                     modern offshore oil and gas industry seeks to
                     understand the complex system of patterns that form a
                     reservoir.  It does so because it needs to maximise the
                     reservoir's potential, and reduce its risks.  The
                     challenge today is the optimum flow from a reservoir
                     in complete safety.

## Fig. 18. Page from a documentary treatment.

Risks are for pioneers.

DISSOLVE TO:

SEQUENCE 3.      The title PATTERNS and beneath it the words a film for Total Oil Marine and the Company symbol. The titles are accompanied by an original piece of music.

DISSOLVE TO:

SEQUENCE 4.      We are looking at water. A slight breeze ruffles the surface. We are in sufficient close up so that it is unclear whether the water is part of a large mass or a small pond. The camera pulls back to reveal an ornamental pond in the centre of an open square. We are in Paris, in front of Total's Ile de France offices. Our central character, Daniel Picard, walks into the picture from the right and proceeds towards the offices. We hear him say in voice over:

"I first started to work on Alwyn North in 1981 at Total in Paris. Previously I had been working on the Frigg system in the North Sea, where we had been involved principally in the transportation of gas. Alwyn represented a opportunity for us now to become oil and gas producers. That was the challenge."

CUT TO:

SEQUENCE 5.      The glass doors to the offices. Daniel Picard pushes them open and walks in. He nods to the reception and they smile in reply. He is obviously well known.

He walks across to the lift and we see him press the button. We cut to the display panel. It flashes Rez de Chausee and then we see the number 1,2,3, ..., as we do the V/O continues.

## Fig. 18. Page from a documentary treatment (continued).

predominantly science based subjects without some basic science education and interest.

If writing for a television audience is your primary ambition, the BBC, the ITV companies and their equivalent anywhere in the world, may still have sizeable documentary departments, sometimes broken down into subject areas such as arts and music, science or current affairs. Although they may still maintain a permanent staff which may include researchers, writers and writer/directors (a common combination in documentaries), increasingly they employ freelance people for specific programmes or series of programmes. And with the tendency to de-regulate television in Britain and pressure to employ independent production companies, their role becomes more important.

## Independents

Some confusion may arise over the term 'independent'. When the BBC's monopoly ended in the 1950s, television companies that relied on advertising for their revenue were called Commercial Television Contractors and each was responsible for supplying programmes for different parts of the United Kingdom, although they often banded together, as they still do, to provide programmes for the entire network.

Gradually, as franchises changed, these companies came to be known as the Independent Television companies, although their independence was ultimately controlled by the advertisers and, it could be argued, that the BBC, supported only by the licence fee, was strictly more independent. But the name ITV has stuck and the real 'independents' (or **'indies'** as they're sometimes called) are the production companies set up by producer/impresarios with directors perhaps and varying from a basic administrative structure to quite elaborate organisations with their own technical facilities. (See also Chapter 3 on Commercials.)

So, in addition to seeking work as a writer in the BBC or ITV companies where competition for jobs is high, you would be advised to concentrate also on the independent production companies, finding out what subjects they have produced or are preparing. The names appear in the directories listed in the Appendix but as with commercials, studying the trade papers is useful. *Screen International* and *Broadcast* are the best known.

## Channel Four

There is another good reason for approaching the independent companies. When Channel Four started, many producers and directors left the BBC and ITV to set up their own companies, for Channel Four, uniquely in Britain, is like a publisher. It does not produce its own programmes, broadly, but commissions independent companies, and sometimes the ITV companies too, to produce on its behalf. This does not always amount to 100% finance, however, and increasingly co-productions or complicated deals with pre-sales to other countries arranged by the production company are the ways that programmes are packaged and this certainly includes documentaries. This also applies to Channel Five and others like the History Channel.

## Independents widen the net

The proliferation of independents and the long drawn out negotiations for setting up programmes meant that they had to turn to the production of specialised subjects for non-theatrical audiences as well.

Similarly, companies who had built their reputations on the production of these types of films and videos, went to Channel Four with ideas for programmes often with great success. Luckily the sub-contracting to independents of programmes, including documentaries, by the BBC and ITV, led to a greater expansion, albeit with more competition, in the independent sector than in other areas of film or television.

## Selling your idea

As always with getting a foothold as a writer, for whatever audience, it is the basic idea that is the most important. And in the case of documentaries, as well as originality, there must be practicality.

So, for example, if you have an idea for an advanced driver training series which might appeal to an oil company as a sponsor, it would pay to research the type of productions that particular oil companies have made and then approach the production companies who have made programmes for them.

Similarly, if you have an idea for a particular science subject, approach the producer in the BBC or ITV that currently is responsible for a science series. Single documentaries are generally more difficult to sell on television everywhere in the world, so it is usually better to slant your idea towards an existing or proposed series. But, probably, best of all, is to try to get an independent production company interested in your idea.

The ideas for sponsored films or corporate videos as they may now be called, largely though not exclusively originate from the client or sponsor who commissions the work, signs a contract and therefore owns the copyright and the material. Like commercials, very often films or videos may have to fit in with overall sales or public relations policy using other media. Production schedules can also be very tight.

## Other starting points in documentaries

One entry point for which there may be vacancies is for researchers. In the corporate sector, researchers are normally used for highly technical or obscure subjects but in television, researchers are more common. The actual job and all the ancillary ones are well covered in a BBC publication:

■ *The Television Researchers' Guide* by Kathy Chater obtainable from BBC Publications.

So if you have qualifications in any specialised subjects or merely an inquisitive, persistent and orderly mind, the job of researcher in documentaries is a good introduction to script writing. A word of warning however; researchers are expected to come up with facts, contacts and visual possibilities. They are not expected to suggest to the writer the shape of the script, unless this is done with the utmost tact and diffidence.

Researchers engaged on highly technical or unusual subjects, however, may be asked to move forward to writing a script and this has even been known to result in their directing also, if only because they are the only people around who know enough about the subject to be able to work amicably with experts! Finally, as an outsider if you can put up an idea to a producer and introduce a sponsor or some finance, you will always be welcome.

OFFSHORE CITY.


A proposal for a
50 minute documentary
film.


© LMN Films and Roland Brinton.

---

One day large numbers of people will live
permanently in space.

Many space stations will orbit the earth.
Factories, laboratories, communication centres
and all the backup for those who work in them.
These space age commuters will travel between
stations by shuttle, dressed in survival suits
as a precaution.

Each individual in this hostile environment will
represent the top of a mighty pyramid of
effort. They will have to be sustained by massive
physical resources backed by an organisation
of immense complexity.

The blueprint for this is already being drawn
in the imagination of future-planners. The
reality exists too.......in the offshore city.

---

INTRODUCTION.


For the next six months up to 700 men will be living and working on a
patch of sea 100 miles east of Shetland. Out there are two oil/gas
platforms under construction, a massive crane-barge for the heavy lifts
and a semi-submersible floating hotel plus a whole fleet of support
vessels. There are three heli-decks, two helicopters for internal flights
and regular schedule to and from 'the beach' - the Scottish mainland.

To go there for the first time is to 'go abroad'. You check in at a
terminal with ticket and passport. Details of next of kin and blood
group are swallowed by the computer, 'in the unlikely event.....'.
You are searched, survival-suited and put into a bright red helicopter
complete with muzak and a pilot with a reassuring voice.

## Fig. 19. Research and proposals for a documentary about life on an oil rig.

After two hours or so you spot activity on the horizon of the heaving
sea. Once down the disc of the heli-deck turns out to be more substantial
than you first thought. You check in again, terse hostel style, and with
room-key, luggage and a small information pack you find your cabin.
It is shared, barren of all but the most functional home comforts and
very, very clean. It is probably a bit like a modern Swedish jail cell
and it is going to be home for the next two weeks.

Your information pack contains a very handy little rule book to help
you avoid being deported or killed prior to your scheduled departure.
It also tells you that meal-times are every four hours around the clock.
The food servery presents a mind blowing variety show in quantities
beyond belief. Next to you someone is eating a stack of three T-bones
to be followed by a salad bowl enough for a family. All around are
Portuguese, Spaniards, French, Dutch, German, Scots and English, all
hungry and all male.

So this is not the Club Med and off you go, by helicpter again, to
a 12 hour work-shift...........finding comfort perhaps in the familiarity
of something you have done before.

---

## PROPOSAL.

In general our proposal is for a 50 minute documentray film about life
and work offshore. We think the subject can be viewed by the audience
on a combination of three levels.

Those of us who have worked out there are always being asked what it is
like. The North Sea oil story is not new but what has changed since the
frontier days is the scale and the confidence of what is happening.
The new offshore city is an island, self reliant and powerful, using
satellites for contact with the outside world, taking supplies from land
as imports and exporting the oil and gas in return. This very self-
sufficiency somehow increases the sense of isolation.

The first level of our proposal is for a general interest 'experience'
of the offshore city from a subjective point of view.

Just as with space the volume of physical, technical and logistic backup
is largely taken for granted in life offshore. The individual worker
is the visible tip of the iceberg.

Paying scant attention to the process of oil and gas production the second
level of our proposal is that we should look at the organisation of men
and technology which makes the whole venture possible. Insight for this
would be found in Aberdeen, London, Paris and Rotterdam with the final
responsibility coming to rest on the shoulders of those running the
system offshore.

The final part of our proposal is for a look to the future.

This, the largest of the offshore cities, is also probably the last to
be created in this part of the world. It is too expensive in men and
resources to be repeated for the marginal fields that remain. A new,
less massive technology is on the way.

The lessons learned need not be lost and the present experience could
well form the basis for the future of large scale operations in hostile.
environments far from home. As an ending for our programme it would
not be too fanciful to make comparisons with the problems which will have
to be solved to make a future in space a reality.

**Fig. 19. Research and proposals for a documentary
about life on an oil rig (continued)**

## Production starting points

With the other technical jobs in other departments – production, camera, sound, editing (film or video), the same advice applies as with previous chapters on commercials and feature films. But again, it is a matter of research to find the departments of the BBC, ITV or the independent production companies who are active in the area that interests you most.

As with commercials, most independent production companies have a permanent set-up, however modest, and therefore the runner, tea person, secretarial route in is often as good as any but obviously for the more technical departments like camera, sound and editing, film school training can again put you at an advantage (see Chapter 7 on Training).

The growth of Business TV Networks may provide opportunities for newcomers, in which case you will need to approach production companies who specialise in this kind of work.

## Art direction

Art direction and design form a less important part of documentaries, although some fictionalised story lines may be incorporated. Historical reconstruction, for example, or even quite elaborate dramatic sequences or complete productions when what may still be called a documentary becomes in production terms akin to a feature film or television drama; the films of John Cleese demonstrating sales techniques are good examples.

## Normal size of a documentary production crew

The more usual documentary film approach only differs from the production of feature films and commercials in size, scope, schedule and budget. This means that in overall charge of the production is certainly a producer.

If the company is handling more than one project in parallel, even if not actually in production at the same time, there will be a production manager. Of course, a director may well have done his own research, treatment (see Figure 1) and script. An assistant director (sometimes on documentaries called a unit manager or personal assistant (PA)) does the detailed organisation both before and during shooting. This is a very important job on documentaries as with more restricted budgets, the assistant becomes in addition a public relations person for the company, dealing both with people and facilities on location and guarding the budget and schedule. Transport, meals and accommodation are also his responsibility as is the general contentment of everybody concerned with the production. This is sometimes a delicate balancing act, bearing in mind that he is, even if a freelance, basically a company person answerable to the production manager and producer.

## Technical jobs on a documentary

The camera department normally consists of a cameraman who is responsible for lighting, if applicable, exposure and normally does his own operating (see Camera Operator Feature Films page 25). He has one camera assistant who does the jobs of focus puller and clapper/loader (see Feature Films page 25) and both are responsible for the camera equipment which may include a lightweight dolly (even a wheelchair can be used) and this is operated by whoever can be most spared.

If lighting is at all elaborate, one or more electricians are employed, not only to install and adjust lights but to link up to mains supplies and guard against overloading.

The sound department often reduces to one sound recordist who operates the tape recorder, places microphones in position, adjusts neck or radio mikes or handles a microphone during the shot. With elaborate camera movement and complicated dialogue scenes, it may be advisable for quality and speed to employ a boom swinger or operator similar to a feature film.

The editing staff on film consists of an editor with one assistant editor who may be engaged by the company for one film or be permanently employed by the company. Equally, as with commercials, editing may be sub-contracted to an editing service specialising in documentaries.

The actual editing of a filmed documentary follows exactly similar patterns to feature films (page  41).

## DOCUMENTARIES ON VIDEO

With documentaries originating on video, the numbers on a production crew can be even more modest. Production is normally carried out with one camera recording a single scene at a time as in film and the schedule arranged similarly (for multi-camera TV see Chapter 6 on Television).

### Documentary video production crew

The unit will consist normally of a director who may not have

Salalah and Nadj sequences showing (a) Over use of Salalah plan water resources and (b) Waste of ancient water in the Nadj. (Note: not yet visited).

Out on the Nadj a bore hole pours water onto the desert. This is followed by shots of young trees being watered by bowser along a road (Nizwah – Salalah).

> However hard we try, Oman will never be turned green – except by Nature. The harder we try the greater will be our disappointment when we fail. Some are already being disappointed.

Shots of bowsers delivering water to new homes in Nizwah.

> New Homes in Nizwah can no longer be connected to piped water. They have much in common with the ten kilometres of young palms on the road to Salalah. Both are being supplied by bowsers.

Pictorial examples of small scale pollution such as cars being washed in the Wadi.

> This illustrates the need for a set of priorities – many of which are obvious when you remember that water moves by gravity to the lowest possible level and carries with it much of what it collects on the way down.

Dramatic shots of the Copper mine at Wadi Souq. We see the tailings dam, the chemical deposits and the run off.

> With less water than more temperate lands the impact of pollution on desert countries is much greater. The sun takes up the water leaving only the poison.

The brown, green and acid yellow crystals of the settling pond fill the screen.

> A single coffee cup of this would kill you.

A group of farmers enjoying coffee together as they look out over fertile terraces. At a spring in the mountains a boy watches the water as it sparkles from the rocks.

> The water is at its best when it starts its journey to the sea. Even these days, our first use of it is in the traditional way.

We follow the water as it moves through the falaj system. It takes us back to the group of men with their coffee cups. They are in discussion.

> Those who manage the falaj hold the life of the community in their hands. Taking that responsibility gives them the power to dictate the way in which the water is distributed.

Scenes in the village gardens show channels in the falaj being opened and closed. Children play in it while the women do their washing.

**Fig. 20. Page from a documentary treatment.**

the luxury of an assistant director. If the director has moved from television, he may have a PA (personal assistant) who acts more as a secretary, the director doing the administrative chores himself both during reconnaissance and during the actual shooting.

The video cameraman is responsible for all jobs concerned with the camera including the lighting unless this is very elaborate. The technical line-up of the equipment is, however, in the hands of an engineer who may also record the sound, although with other than very simple shooting, a sound recordist is still advisable. An additional job of the engineer is to note the time codes on the videotape of each shot, which is the equivalent of the clapper/loader and script supervisor recording scenes and footages in film. The PA or director will also keep a log of all scenes recorded (see Figure 21 page 109). And, as budgets get tighter, the one person crew who does everything, can now be seen!

## Video editing

The editing of videotape starts with making a copy of the master tape, incorporating the time code for identification and carrying out the initial editing on to a third tape **'off line'**.

Many film editors have learned to operate off line equipment for creatively they are doing precisely the same job, the difference being that film is physically cut and joined to the next scene and you can see the actual images in the hand whereas on tape the editing is electronic and the tape is never actually cut but transferred to another piece of tape and can only be viewed on a monitor.

**VIDEO LOG**

| PROD NO. | | DATE | TAPE NO. | SHEET NO |
|---|---|---|---|---|
| TITLE LOG. BP. Miller. | | | ① | ① |
| CLIENT | | | | |

| SCENE | TIMECODE/TAPE TIME | | G/NG TAKE | COMMENTS |
|---|---|---|---|---|
| | START | FINISH | | |
| | | | | |
| #1 Leith Pier Coat | | | | |
| 12.10.          1-1 | 01.00.39. — | W on Bay Tit — lag. | | |
| | 01. 01. 55 | piers out. Bay / barge. | | |
| | 01. 03. — | piers side shot ) (Lag + Bay | | |
| | 01. 04. 10. | C/u W. Leith i.e. | | |
| | | Mq machine crane s. | | |
| | 01. 05. 37 | car pan piers out barge | | |
| | 01. 07. 00. | Lag Ang. | | |
| | 01. 07. 30. | Sh.h Bays | | |
| | 01. 08. 00. | Rd Lag ut stop. | | |
| | | Piers on. | | |
| | 01. 09. 50 | C/u car bring sink ( blue) | | |
| | 01. 10. 50. | s/u c car. Lag away. | | |
| | 01. 11. 31 | on ship Mc Brack fras 0.4 | | |
| | 01. 12. 36 | Lads ship Deck | | |
| | 01. 12. 62 | M/S W Avalt crane | | |
| | 01. 13. 10 | C/u Deck Hd. p/o M/S Deck | | |
| | 01. 14. 30. | B/S Deck Hd. + Sith | | |
| | 01. 14. 25. | Crane ship some above. L W.C. | | |
| | 01. 15. 60. | Attach crane | | |
| | 01. 17. 10. | Lift piers. | | |
| | 01. 18. 50. | c/u crane Gab | | |
| | 01. 19. 20. | End). | | |
| | | | | |
| | | | | |
| | | | | |

**Fig. 21. Documentary video log sheet.**

## Non-linear editing

To speed up and achieve great accuracy and flexibility, off-line editing can be carried out on computers which transfer the master (film or tape) to computer hard discs. The big advantage of this system is that you have instant access to any section of the captured material and can review different takes or edits side by side. When the off-line edit is completed, the final EDL (Edit Decision List) which includes all the time codes is used in the on-line edit to auto assemble both picture and audio cuts; this greatly reduces the time and thus the cost of the on-line stage of post-production.

## Off-line editing

Off-line editing, which is the equivalent on film of editing to rough cut stage, is carried out by off-line editors who develop tremendous dexterity operating the equipment and making up the equivalent of a cutting copy (see Chapter 2 on Feature films). This initial edit from the different tapes or discs can be done faster than film editing.

Adding this to the cheaper cost of the master tape and the elimination of developing and printing means that overall costs up to this stage of production can be considerably less than film. But there is still the matter of size of screen and the numbers in the audience for showings of the finished production to bear in mind when considering the pros and cons of film and video.

## Video editing – the final stages

It is the next stage of video production where costs can run away most alarmingly. Having convinced everybody – produ-

cer, director, commissioning editor in the case of TV programmes produced by independents, sponsor in corporate
videos – that the off-line version is satisfactory, the final tidying
up and precision editing, together with the insertion of titles
and any special visual effects are done in the on-line suite
which may, in some cases, be merely a sophisticated extension
of the off-line equipment.

## On-line editing

This operation which in film terms is a combination of fine
cutting, making and cutting in of opticals and titles, some
sound mixing and negative cutting to production of an answer
print (see Chapter 2 on Feature films, post-production) is all
being done electronically and instantaneously (see Figure 15
page 55).

By instantaneously is meant a matter of hours rather than the
weeks it might take on film. The effectiveness of this operation
is in the hands of the **on-line** editor. This job not only demands
extensive knowledge of the equipment's capabilities, which
may be constantly modified and updated to provide extra
facilities, but also dexterity in 'hands on' operation and creative
instincts for the general tempo and effectiveness of the
programme.

Of course, just as in film dubbing, the director and off-line
editor will have their own ideas as to what they want to achieve;
but there can still be a considerable additional creative input
from the on-line editor.

It is this skill and experience, combined with the enormous cost
of the equipment, housed usually in a fairly luxurious and

conveniently placed location, that makes the rental cost so high for these on-line suites and where every unscheduled hour can play havoc with the budget.

As well as carrying out the final editing, what is also being done is going back to the original master tape and transferring to a new master, incorporating all the details for the finished production. It is from this master that further copies will be made for transmission on television, for showing in non-theatrical situations or for bulk release on video or DVD including rental or sale.

## Other jobs in an on-line edit suite

The production staff in an on-line edit suite can be quite extensive. The on-line editor may have one assistant who is responsible for title and caption generation. Other video assistants provide back up with operating tape machines and subsequently making copies and filing and recording material.

Here, once again, are all the administrative jobs which include that of handling the bookings of the editing suite (often a great juggle to keep impatient clients happy), secretarial, book-keeping and the ubiquitous runner, gofer or tea person.

The stress that can build up sometimes during long editing sessions which stretch on into the night, means that whoever is responsible for providing liquid refreshment of any sort is a very welcome member of the company. And as always with this starting point, a chance for any newcomer to see precisely what the technical jobs entail and to get to know people in production.

## STARTING POINTS IN DOCUMENTARIES

If you are keen to get into the production of documentaries on film or video, the same advice applies in the different departments as with feature films (Chapter 2) and commercials (Chapter 3).

Obviously, in the case of video, some knowledge of video equipment either through training or hands on experience even as an amateur with cameras and editing will help to prove to any potential employer your dedication and keenness to be involved in professional production.

So it is a question of research in directories and concentrating on companies that make documentaries or post-production companies that provide editing facilities in film or video to documentary companies.

Getting started in the BBC or ITV companies is another matter and will be dealt with in Chapter 7 on training.

## SUMMING UP

Working in documentaries covers a very wide range of subject and production techniques.

- Those made on film have many similarities, as far as jobs are concerned, with features and commercials although with smaller crews.

- Those made on video have many similarities to both film and video techniques, so it is hopefully becoming clear that there is a deal of cross-fertilization possible both in production and in technique.

What this means is that people starting in film documentaries may move in some cases to feature films or commercials and back again. Less likely, but still theoretically possible, is to move from television documentaries to television drama.

There is a very go-ahead organisation DFG (Documentary Film Making Group) which offers advice on training and other aspects of the genre. Contact them at: 4th Floor, Shacklewell Studios, 28 Shacklewell Lane, London E8 2EZ. Tel: (020) 7249 6600. *www.dfgdocs.com.*

# 5

# Animation

Basically, animation is the recording on film or video of drawings, clay or plasticine figures like Nick Park's Wallace and Gromit or any object one or two frames at a time, with the movement being changed for each frame so that when the complete action is projected or transmitted, it gives the impression of continuous movement.

Animation is still best known through the cartoon films of Walt Disney, and from *Tom and Jerry* to *The Simpsons*. Unfortunately, the enormous cost of production caused by the labour intensive nature of the work means that outlets in cinemas are now limited to feature productions like Shrek or *Finding Nemo*. But animation continues to be popular in a variety of forms in commercials, on television programmes and for video and DVD release (*The Wrong Trousers*).

## PRODUCTION

The production of conventional animation usually starts with a storyboard (see Figure 22 page 116) which is similar to a storyboard used for live action commercials except that the drawings may be done by the artist who is going to do the final artwork.

Fig. 22. Storyboard for an animation sequence.

116

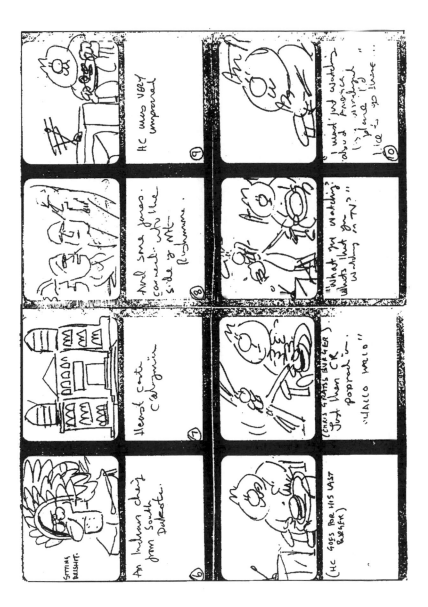

Unlike live action, the first stage of production is the recording, editing and final mixing of the sound track which is prepared to an exact timing (in the case of commercials, this means down to single frames).

This is carried out using the same techniques as feature films, documentaries and commercials.

## The animation studio

The first jobs here are the preparation of bar sheets, dope sheets and layouts (see Figures 23 and 24, pages 120, 121) which are really the equivalent of shooting scripts with the exact information for the artists so that they can follow the action. The animation is drawn on paper punched to register on to pegs so that each successive drawing can be accurately aligned.

The artists who work on all the drawings, which are normally painted on transparent cells also punched with holes to keep each picture exactly in register, are called **trace and paint artists**.

Different artists will be responsible for the background, middle ground or foreground but all the cells have to remain in register and checkers may be employed to check the progress of the scenes.

Sequences can be tried out on video with print outs and live action video might be recorded and examined in detail before any drawings are done to check the movement of animals for example.

## Photographing the action

When all the cells have been completed for a scene or sequence, they are passed to a rostrum cameraman who operates a rostrum camera. The rostrum is usually vertically mounted and has to be built in to rock steady foundations.

Following the bar and dope sheets, the cells are now photographed frame by frame mounted precisely on the register pins similar to the ones on which they were drawn.

This is a time consuming job requiring care, orderliness and patience. Although there are some automated and computerised short cuts it is still pretty labour intensive and it is good going to complete on average 20–30 seconds screen time per day.

Whatever the final release of the production, the rushes will be sent to the film laboratory for developing and printing. The print will then be synchronised with the sound track and any cuts made similar to editing a feature film or commercial in a cutting room.

If the final release is on film, the completion process is really similar to feature films with the negative being cut in the laboratory to match the cutting copy (see page 57) with a combined print being produced.

If the release is for television or video, the completion will be similar to television commercials with a clean print being transferred to video for completion in an on-line edit suite.

## STARTING POINTS IN ANIMATION

Without art school training, you will have to convince any potential employer of your talent as an artist in the particular style for which the animator you have approached is known. There are cases of people who have started drawing and

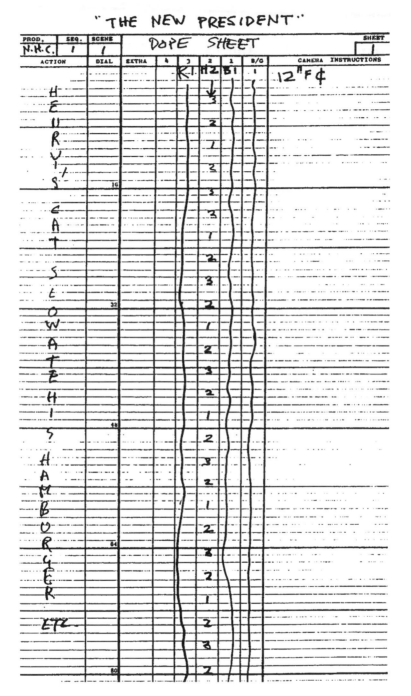

**Fig. 23. Dope sheet (animation shooting script).**

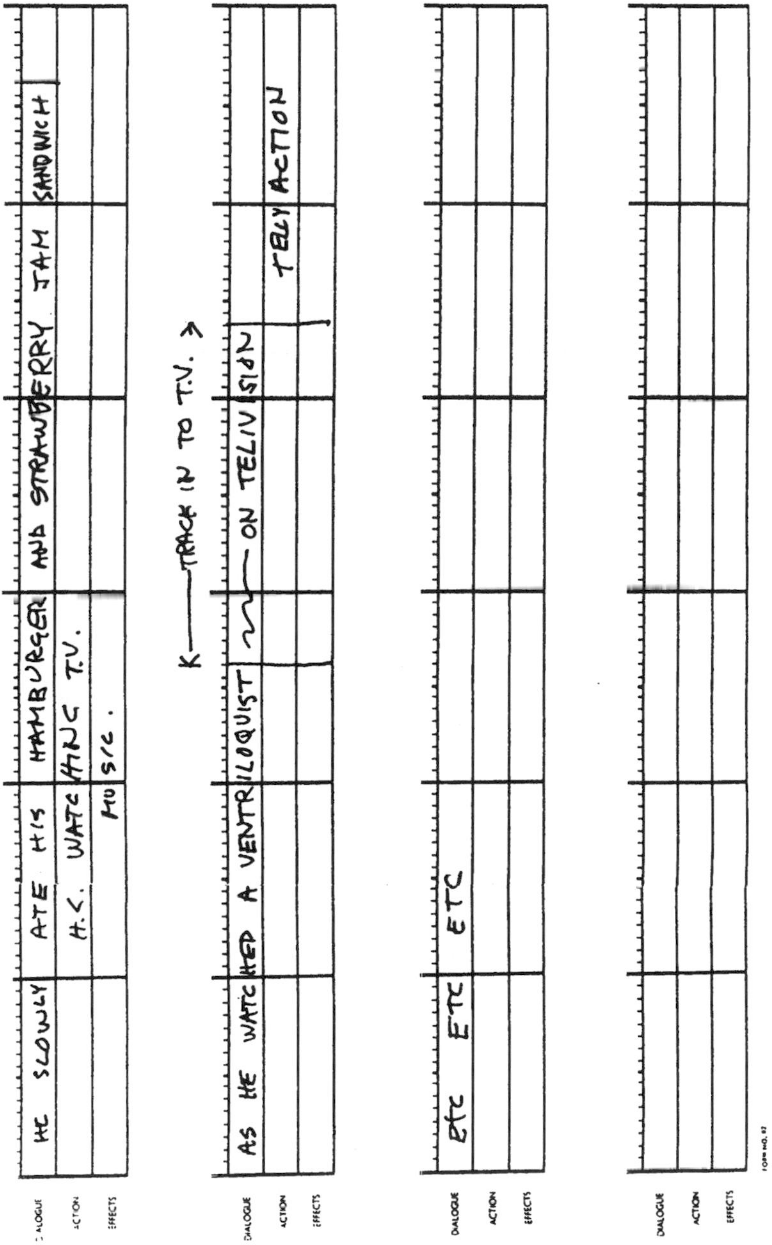


Fig. 24. Bar sheet (animation shooting script).

making their own animation films at home at the age of fourteen, like Nick Park, but they are a pretty rare talent.

Graduates from art school could try to get work in an animation studio in any capacity and progress from there. So competitive are the vacancies that art school graduates should even be prepared to start in a company doing office work or as the ubiquitous runner or tea person in order to get experience.

There are a number of film schools where there is an option to do animation and even some where it is possible to obtain a degree in animation. With these qualifications, you at least have a showreel of your work from which it is easy to see your particular style. But if you are considering computer animation, it is essential to do a foundation course in basic animation.

Many students and aspiring animators only consider their drawing or modelling techniques when applying for jobs as an animator. Of equal importance to the drawing of the animation is the detailed *timing* of each action – especially ANTICIPATION which gently leads the viewer into the proceeding action – or *no* anticipation to create a surprise or shock.

A smooth action is produced by a slow start, gently speeding up and then a slow down to a cushioned stop. One simple example of speeding up and slowing down is the 'BOUNCING BALL'. The dropping ball gains speed until it hits the ground where it squashes, then immediately stretches to bounce back up again, losing its stretch and speed as it reaches the height of the bounce. The action is repeated on a declining scale until it eventually rolls along the ground – or *surprise*, a booted leg enters the screen and kicks it – or *anticipation*...cut to a wider shot to include a character preparing to kick the rolling ball.

So once again it is a matter of studying the directories listed in the Appendix and following the advice in Chapter 8, Selling Yourself, with the added advantage that you can produce if required examples of your work if you are called for an interview.

A good book which explains the principles of animation is *The Animator's Survival Kit* by Richard Williams published by Faber & Faber.

## COMPUTERISED ANIMATION

Most animators consider that traditional cell animation still gives the greatest degree of artistic creativity.

Recently, however, there have been so many advances in computer animation that a new breed of animator has been born. For example, effects can now be produced digitally on disc thus making transfer back to film or video possible. *The Lord of the Rings* trilogy are good examples. So for art students, graphics and computer training is more than ever required to operate a variety of image manipulation systems like Flame or Harry.

### Harry

**Harry** is the manufacturer's name of a device for creating a mass of original visual effects, either from scratch or by manipulating existing material or a combination of both.

It can be used as a back up to conventional animation, for example, by electronically eliminating strings and supports in puppets or model work thus saving time during the actual shooting.

It can be used for rectifying mistakes in the original material by 'painting in' other images, also for obliterating backgrounds and matting in new ones frame by frame, a technique done for many years in films by special effects departments and by film laboratories, but at some length and labour. In machines like Harry, this can be done in a matter of hours but only, it must be remembered, on video or disc for subsequent transfer to film.

Outrageous effects and colours, and metamorphosing ('morphing'), that is changing the shapes of people or objects, manipulation of colour to turn spring into autumn, in fact virtually any form of special effect is possible.

Harry can be used for marrying conventional animation with electronically created 3D animation and adding more visual effects. For example, a conventional cell animation sequence of a boy walking down a street which has been created electronically, could be mixed together. A space ship roars down the street (again created electronically) and snatches up the boy. The whole scene is then enhanced by the Harry operator by adding smoke coming up from a manhole in the street and flames belching from the back of the space ship.

And all this could have been done equally by marrying live action shots or a combination of live action and animation.

## Working on Harry

Harry operators sometimes have an assistant to back them up in what can be a drawn out and tiring process and tape operators are on hand to record the finished product and make copies of the master, just as in an on-line edit suite.

As this whole process is a mixture of editing and original creation of effects, some experience of video editing is an advantage and knowledge of graphic design helpful.

Although the manufacturers of Harry run training courses for operators, they would be unlikely to give places to outsiders not working for facilities companies owning their equipment. But if you are working in any capacity as a tape operator, a runner or receptionist in a video post-production company, you might well persuade your employers to release you for a course.

The expense and constant modification of equipment like Harry means that recognised training establishments may not have the resources to own such a facility.

## GRAPHICS

An extension or alternative to animation is the field of graphics but with the common advisability of acquiring training and qualifications at art college or courses in graphic design.

As with all areas of film and television, getting a job is highly competitive and, in graphics, possibly more so on account of the large numbers qualifying each year from the great many colleges and Universities.

### What does graphics cover?

Graphics is basically the design and production of main (front) and end credit titles of films and TV programmes of every type.

The cheapest or most specialised sponsored film or corporate video may call merely for computer generated titles from the choice of fonts available in the on-line edit suite.

The other end of the scale might be the design of a completely new lettering style incorporated into complete sequences of animation or live action for a major international feature film. The design of the main title, that is the actual title of the film, may be used also in advertising and promotion and thus become the logo for the film. Who does not recognise instantly the 007 insignia?

As has been said previously, features are still largely made on 35mm film, so all the design and photography of titles is really similar to animation. The incorporation of the titles with the background therefore becomes a job done optically either in a laboratory or by companies that specialise in the complete production of titles.

The design and making of trailers is another specialised form of production incorporating graphics.

These title companies who may also do animation, are listed in directories in the Appendix.

## Graphics for commercials

A vast amount of graphics is featured in commercials and here the graphics designer has to liaise closely with the advertising agency for lettering style may have to echo that of advertising in other media.

## Graphics for television

Every type of programme plus trailers and 'promos' call for graphics of some sort again, as with films, varying from the simplest main and end credit titles to elaborate mini-productions using the most sophisticated computer generated animation and special visual effects.

In the body of the programme, there may be elaborate diagrams and explanatory graphics which may have been carried out by conventional animation or be computer generated and either pre-recorded or live, in the case of news type programmes.

## Starting points in graphics

Whatever area of film or television graphics interests you most, it is unlikely that you could be considered for the most junior job of Graphic Design Assistant without some qualification from art college or University which included graphics and that means a thorough knowledge of all lettering styles, contemporary and historical.

Increasingly in video, some experience of computerised graphics and visual effects is an advantage and some experience in a graphic design company may be advisable.

Nevertheless, some ITV companies who have their own graphics departments and specialised independent companies may prefer to take people straight from college and train them 'in house' or arrange for them to go on courses.

Graphics is such a specialised area of production, that it is unlikely that the tea person/runner route could lead to working in graphics without training, in fact the opposite could be the case: a really dedicated and determined graduate might well be prepared to take a very lowly job in order to get the feel of the whole production process and get to know the people involved.

So consult the directories listed in the Appendix and follow the advice in Chapter 8, Selling Yourself. One distinct advantage in both animation and graphics is that you can offer to produce a portfolio of your work which provides instant evidence of your style and talent.

With the enormous growth in digitally produced graphics, animation and special effects, computer knowledge and experience is essential as well.

## DVD

This stands for digital video disc and it is where the long-term future of all types of film production probably lies. When professional cameras can use sufficiently high quality DVD, then there will be no need to transfer to any other material for editing and subsequent release. The completed master DVD would then be transmitted via satellite and stored, ready for screening in the cinema or wherever, thus doing away with the cumbersome transport of film in containers.

But one thing is sure: whether the future sounds the death knell of film stock and processing and is replaced by small and convenient DVD or its equivalent, *there will always be the need for talented and skilled technicians at every stage of any production.*

# 6

# Television

In spite of some differences in the names of technicians' jobs in film and television and even differences between various ITV companies and the BBC, there are many elements of production that are common to all types of film and TV programmes.

Many documentary series like travel or wildlife may be produced almost entirely on film and transferred to video or DVD in the final on-line editing and transmitted on tape. Current affairs programmes normally originate on single camera videotape but may, if the subject matter is hard news, incorporate some element of live television, perhaps via satellite link, or studio sequences pre-recorded just prior to transmission.

Some drama programmes may be produced on a single camera on film or recorded scene by scene on tape with subsequent off- and on-line editing using basically similar techniques as described in Chapter 4 on Documentaries.

## AREAS UNIQUE TO TELEVISION

But there are three areas of programming which are virtually unique to television production and have different technical jobs and names, so some of these will be described in greater detail to help you in your choice of career.

They are:

1. Drama, comedy series, soap operas, quizzes, chat shows, 'fly on the wall' type documentaries (often called reality TV), makeover programmes and light entertainment.

2. Sport and Outside Broadcasts (OBs or Events).

3. News programmes.

Numbers 1 and 2 may all use multi-camera techniques and certain of them like chat shows, sport and OBs of actual events may be transmitted live rather than pre-recorded.

In the case of some comedy series, quizzes, chat shows and light entertainment, they are recorded as far as possible all the way through with breaks for commercials (if applicable), for big costume or set changes or if things go terribly wrong. The one thing that is common to all these programmes is that they are recorded with an audience of perhaps several hundred in the studio.

It is generally accepted that this makes for a livelier show more akin to theatre and produces more genuine reaction, in spite of all the technical paraphernalia obstructing some of the view. But the audience will have TV monitors on which they can see the picture that is actually being recorded.

Soaps and some comedy series will usually be pre-recorded in sequences and then edited later for transmission, but in the United States comedy series like *Friends* are still recorded straight through with an audience as they always used to be in the UK.

## Production of a typical 30-minute show

As an example of a multi-camera 'live' programme, here is the schedule for the production of a thirty-minute show in a comedy series.

## Pre-recorded multi-camera production of a half-hour programme

### Scripts

Scripts for a comedy series usually start with a synopsis of all the episodes, similar to a film treatment, giving an outline of the plot and characters but with no detailed dialogue. With unknown writers, a sample dialogue script might be requested for one episode.

At this stage, a story editor or script editor may be engaged to ensure that there is consistency in the characters throughout, especially if different writers are working on the series.

### Design and casting: the director

The director starts work with a synopsis and dialogue script and in parallel briefs the designer and casting director who will line up a selection of actors for the director to cast. The designer will be working with a property buyer who arranges to acquire props and furnishings, and with a head of construction regarding the building of sets.

### Rehearsals

When the cast has been agreed, rehearsals can begin. These take place in specially designed rehearsal rooms or rented halls and, at this stage, the sets are only indicated on the floor with stickytape; makeshift props like tables and chairs with hand props like telephones or teacups will be used.

The production crew will now consist of the director, a PA (production assistant), the floor manager, who is the equivalent of a stage manager in a theatre and perhaps an assistant floor manager.

## The camera script

After three days' rehearsal, the director will write a camera script (see Figure 25 page 134). This is the equivalent of a shooting script for a feature film except that the director will be handling at least four cameras which have to be plotted individually to keep the action going continuously and moving from one set up to another.

If the script calls for any location or library shots, these will be recorded or obtained beforehand and edited so as to be ready for inserting at the actual recording of the whole show in the studio. Technically, the location work is similar to that described in Chapter 4 concerning documentaries on video, except that there will be considerably more people involved: actors, make-up and hairdressing, wardrobe, props, transport and catering. It's again similar to a feature film or a TV drama shot scene by scene on a single camera.

In addition to the camera script which will be copied and sent to everybody concerned, the **Floor Manager** will prepare a studio plan with all the camera movements marked. The PA also makes individual camera cards for each camera with all the shots enumerated from the numbers on the camera script. Thus camera 1 may be responsible for shots 1, 5, 7, 11 and so on to the end of the programme.

### *Technical run-through*

The day before moving in to the studio for recording, there will be a technical run through for all four cameramen, the sound supervisor and the vision mixer whose job at the actual recording is to switch from one camera to another at exactly the moment required by the director.

In the studio the day before recording, the lighting supervisor will be lighting the sets and the director will check them with the designer. The director will also check costumes with wardrobe.

The sets are usually built in a line alongside each other with the set where most of the action takes place in the middle. Half the studio will be taken up with raked seats for the audience.

## Recording the show

On the actual studio day, the whole production crew with equipment can start blocking out the action. This can be called plotting but more usually it is given the more jokey phrase of a stagger through.

The crew has now grown to four cameramen with their cameras, three boom operators with booms and microphones, perhaps a cable pusher to ensure the cables do not get tangled, the lighting supervisor or director who does exactly what his title suggests, electricians who actually move and fix the lights to his orders, four scene men, painters, carpenters and a prop man who is now responsible for props in the studio and, in

**HAROLD**
Yes, I know, Dad.

66.                                    1
    MCS ALBERT

**ALBERT** *Eight in one bed;*
Four brothers, two sisters, and my

mum and dad.  They're all dead now.

67.                         2
    MCS HAROLD

**HAROLD**
Yeah, well, they didn't have gas masks

in them days.

68.                    3
    MED. 2s. HAROLD/ALBERT

**ALBERT**
Yeah, eight of us.  Four up one end,

four down the other.  Roll the sheets

back and we'd look like a tin of sardines.

Hard days they were.  Do you know what we

used to have for breakfast?

69.                         2
    MED. 2s. HAROLD/ALBERT

**HAROLD**
Bread and margarine.


**ALBERT**
That's right.  Bread and margarine.

70.                           1    That's all. / In those days bread and
    MCS ALBERT           margarine meant you were poor and hungry,

not fat and frightened of dropping dead of

cholesterol.  We didn't even know what

71.                         2      cholesterol was in them days. /
    MED. 2s. HAROLD/ALBERT  HAROLD:  You don't now.

72.                         3      ALBERT  We couldn't afford it. / The only
    MED. 2s. HAROLD/ALBERT  thing that kept us going was the free

spoonful of malt at school ......... /cont'd

    P/V 2

**Fig. 25. Camera script for television.**

| PAGES | SCENE | ARTISTS | CAMS | SOUND | SHOTS |
|---|---|---|---|---|---|
| 1 | 1: ALBERT'S BEDROOM + OPENING SLIDES (T/Js) | Albert Steptoe | 4A 3A | F/ROD SIG. | 1 & 1A |
| 2-8 | 2. LIVING ROOM/HALL + T/js. | Harold Steptoe Marcia | 1A 2A | A1 | 2-15 |
| 8-9 | 3. HALL/STAIRS | Harold Marcia | 1B | B1 | 16 |

.........................../ PAUSE FOR CAM. 2 to move to Pos. B. & ARTISTS MOVE/ .............

| PAGES | SCENE | ARTISTS | CAMS | SOUND | SHOTS |
|---|---|---|---|---|---|
| 9 | 4. UPSTAIRS LANDING | Harold Marcia | 2B | F/ROD | 17 |
| 9-10 | 5. HAROLD'S BEDROOM | Harold Marcia | 5A 3B | C1 | 18-20 |
| 10. | 6. ALBERT'S BEDROOM | Albert | 2C | F/ROD | 21 |
| 10-11 | 7. HAROLD'S BEDROOM | Harold Marcia | 5A 3B 4B | C1 Slung mic. | 22-23 |
| 11-13 | 8. UPSTAIRS LANDING/ HAROLD'S ROOM | Harold Marcia Albert | 5A 3B 4B | C1 Slung mic. | 24-35 |

........................../RECORDING BREAK:   CAM. 1 to Pos. C. Liv. Rm.
                                                    3 to Pos. C., Liv. Rm
ROLL BACK & MIX                                     2 to Pos. D., Liv. Rm. ...................

| PAGES | SCENE | ARTISTS | CAMS | SOUND | SHOTS |
|---|---|---|---|---|---|
| 14-25 | 9. LIVING ROOM: A.M. | Harold Albert | 3C 1C 2D/E | A1, B1 | 36-97 |

......................../RECORDING BREAK:   CAM. 3 to Pos. D. Bederama   BM. B to Pos. 2
                                                  1 to Pos. D.      "
                                                  2 to Pos. F.      "        ...............

ROLL BACK & MIX

| PAGES | SCENE | ARTISTS | CAMS | SOUND | SHOTS |
|---|---|---|---|---|---|
| 26-40 | 10. "BAYSWATER BEDERAMA" | Harold Albert | 3D 1D 2F | D1 B2 | 98-157 |

......................../RECORDING BREAK:   CAM. 5 to Pos. B. Harold's Bedroom
                                                  3 to Pos. E.      "        "      BM. C to Pos. 2
                                                  4 to Pos. A. Albert's Bedroom BM. B to Pos. 1
                                                  2 to Pos. D.      "        "
                                                  1 to Pos. B  Hall

**Fig. 25. Camera script for television (continued).**

charge overall, the floor manager and probably an assistant floor manager (similar to an assistant stage manager in the theatre).

Unlike film making where the director controls everything from the floor of the studio, in television all the control is from the **gallery** which may not necessarily even overlook the studio.

## The gallery

The gallery is divided into three – the lighting control with the lighting supervisor in one section, the sound supervisor and grams operator to insert extra sound effects or music where required; both these two suites are on either side of the central part of the gallery which contains monitor screens of what each camera is looking at, monitors which show what is being recorded and all the technical controls and communications systems between people in the gallery and all other key production people.

Occupying this part of the gallery are the producer who throughout has been carrying out a similar role of overall responsibility and organisation to any other type of film or programme; the director, PA, vision mixer and the technical operations manager. The latter is a senior engineer who is responsible for the overall technical quality of the picture and sound being transmitted or recorded.

The director 'calls the shots' to the **vision mixer** who switches to the camera set-up and position called by the director. Most experienced vision mixers following rehearsals with the director on the particular show are able to anticipate the cut from one scene to another so that it happens at the precise moment wanted by the director.

## Full dress rehearsal

Rehearsals having taken place throughout the day, if all goes according to schedule, a full dress run normally takes place between 4.30pm and 6.30pm, thus allowing time for a supper break and lining up the cameras to ensure the quality of the picture and sound is exactly right before the recording of the whole show starts in front of an audience between 7.30pm and 8pm.

## The final recording

As many people in the audience will not have been at the recording of a television show before, a 'warm up' person usually tells them what will happen and probably tells a few jokes to get everybody in a relaxed state of mind. They will certainly be encouraged to laugh and may be urged on during the recording but achieving the right sound balance of audience reaction in a comedy show is quite tricky for the sound supervisor and for the director too, if pauses in the action caused by laughter are necessary.

For a half-hour programme, one and a half hours are normally scheduled for recording the whole show from the time the director says, 'Standby studio and mix...' to 'Fade sound and vision.'

## Editing

Provided all has gone well, only fairly straightforward on-line editing is required to cut together the various sections that have been recorded in the studio into which have already been inserted the titles and any pre-recorded sequences on location or library shots.

Some directors record the whole studio final recording on low band videocassette with a time code taken off the master. They can then examine carefully where any tightening up or changes in the action may have to be made, making a note of the time code, thus saving costly time in the on-line edit suite.

At this time, any additional visual effects will be inserted and finally, it may be necessary to make some adjustments to the sound track in a dubbing theatre and insert some additional sound tracks to make the final mix smoother, if changes to the picture have caused abrupt changes in sound level.

This is doing precisely the same operation as in the dubbing theatre with a feature or documentary film except that in the case of television, the bulk of the sound mixing will have been done at the studio recording.

It only remains for copies of the final master videotape to be made for transmission, for videocassettes, DVDs or overseas distribution and so on; these are done in a sound recording transfer suite in exactly the same way as for documentaries or commercials completed on video.

## OUTSIDE BROADCASTS

Outside broadcasts (OBs) differ from other television programmes in that they invariably feature actual events and therefore may be transmitted live or covered and recorded in their entirety for transmission later.

As a rule they tend to use more cameras – eight is pretty normal for events like football matches or the BAFTA Awards Ceremony, but it can go up to as many as 30 on occasions with such universal international appeal as a major State ceremony or sporting event.

The crews on OBs, even if more numerous, are basically the same as any multi-camera shoot in the studio for chat shows, quizzes or comedy series (see page 130).

This means that each camera will have its camera operator and, if a lot of complicated camera movement is involved, cable pushers. Sound operators and floor managers liaise with the scanner or colour mobile control room which will be located in a truck as near the action as possible.

Here, as in the studio but in rather more cramped conditions, will be the three components of engineering, production and sound, manned by the engineering manager in the first, director and vision mixer in the second and sound supervisor in the third, all with their back up staff where necessary.

In another truck nearby will be recording facilities for videotape manned by VT operators and recording engineers.

If it is a live transmission, a third vehicle manned by engineering staff is involved. Their job is to link up with the national communications network or satellite links.

Dependent on the size and complexity of the OB, additional vehicles may be necessary, but, as far as jobs are concerned, they are mostly engineering or sound and videotape recording based.

Working in OBs calls for a lot of travelling with long and irregular hours in all sorts of weather, but it has that basic excitement of show business which only live transmission can give.

## NEWS PROGRAMMES

Television news gathering, as with newspapers, is a 24 hour, 365 days a year operation.

So anybody who is thinking of making a career in television news should rule out any thought of a steady 9 to 5 Monday to Friday existence.

Production techniques are a mixture of documentary video location shooting and outside broadcasts with the additional ingredients of time and portability.

### Time

Even more than in newspapers, television news is dependent on time. Time to record or obtain visuals live by satellite or other link. Time to research existing material from the news organisation's own library or from other sources. Time to edit, write and record the front of camera and voice over narration.

The greatest saving of time recently for everyone concerned with the production of news programmes has been computerisation.

Therefore for anyone interested in working in television news in any capacity, in front of or behind the camera, on location or in the studio, a well developed computer skill must be a distinct asset.

### Portability

**ENG** or electronic news gathering was the term originally given to describe the most portable professional video cameras.

Indeed, all cameras used in news programmes now are lightweight; this means that they can get in anywhere and be operated by one person to record both picture and sound, although a crew of two is the norm to accompany the journalist/ presenter.

## Location editing

This is now a required element for many home and foreign news stories. The development of satellite communications and relatively lightweight edit packs means that editors can travel with their equipment and set up where space and local electricity supplies allow. Some picture editors may be based overseas as well.

Mobile editing vehicles mean that there is a greater mobility in the way editors are deployed.

## Links vehicles

These vehicles, manned by engineering staff, relay pictures recorded or live back to the studio. Similarly, portable satellite ground stations, carried in a few suitcases, can send stories back directly to the studio.

## The news studio

This is equipped with normal studio facilities which may include remotely controlled cameras with prompting equipment.

The studios are staffed by television operators who operate the cameras either direct or by remote control. Other operators act as vision mixers, work video effects equipment, control the lighting and ensure the output is to high technical standards.

Operators also work in the videotape transmission area and copy tapes and film between different formats and world television standards. In addition, they support graphic designers. All in all, these are similar to studio jobs in other programmes but with the difference that they are working generally to very tight schedules and dealing with a great variety of source material.

To a limited extent, news also needs sets and props which may have to be erected and struck to make way for a different programme later the same day.

## Graphics

For most news programmes, electronic paintboxes are used to create captions using an electronic stylus and tablet. These machines give access to various electronic tools such as airbrushes, scalpels, paste and lettering; all these are generated direct on to video.

Designers also use a wide range of sources – 35mm slides, videotape, or live material. Computer graphics can produce simulated three dimensional scenes and all these devices can be stored after they have been made for use during transmission or recording.

Designers work closely with producers, directors, operators and editors. Production time available for a particular job may be a matter of weeks or minutes.

## Journalists

Large numbers of journalists are employed in news pro-grammes. Many will never be seen on the screen, but will work behind the scenes compiling stories. All regions produce local news programmes and people often gain experience here before moving to national news programmes.

When vacancies occur in local news, preference is often given to applicants who know the area. First jobs are either on a freelance basis or as news trainees or researchers.

Many newcomers have English degrees and have then taken courses in journalism before getting practical working experience in newspapers or magazines.

## STARTING POINTS IN TELEVISION

First, having chosen the particular area that interests you most – drama, current affairs, documentaries, news, OBs and so on and which particular department within these you think you are most suited for, there are then three possible starting points in television in Britain.

### 1. BBC
Entry is strictly controlled and formalised both for actual job vacancies and for trainees. Study Chapter 7 on training (BBC), and follow the advice given there.

### 2. ITV
Study Chapter 7 on training (ITV), but if you live in one of the regions there just might be occasional junior posts – secretarial, runners and so on – which could get you a foot in the door.

### 3. Independents
As with other types of production, research is necessary

through the trade papers and directories listed in the Appendix to find out the companies that are most active in the area that interests you most.

## SUMMING UP

Having narrowed down the type of programme and department that you are aiming for, concentrate your efforts there and follow the advice in Chapter 8 on selling yourself.

For engineering and technical operations jobs, it is recommended that you opt for training before applying for jobs (apart from the BBC who provide their own). If you do obtain work in ITV or an independent company as a runner, for example, push very hard to get on a training course or short course.

# 7

# Training for Film and Television

## IMPORTANCE OF THE RIGHT TRAINING

In recent years, opportunities for training in film and television have increased enormously. Unfortunately, possibilities for employment have not increased correspondingly in all areas. Now, more than ever, if you elect for formal training as opposed to starting in any position, however lowly, and working your way up and learning on the job, it is necessary to research the various courses on offer and try to find one that is best for you. Because of the largely freelance nature of work in film and television, obtaining qualifications is no guarantee of employment; entry into both industries, in spite of many attempts at regulation, is still largely haphazard.

## Catch 22

Before changes in the law governing trade unions, the greatest regulator was the fact that employers were unlikely to take on newcomers unless they were members of the appropriate trade union and people could not apply for membership unless they first had a job. This Catch 22 situation led to the growth of a great many ruses, most of which bore no relation to training, qualifications or experience. BECTU (Broadcasting Entertainment Cinematograph and Theatre Union) did guarantee membership to successful students at certain accredited film schools (see list on page 148) but trade union membership was still no guarantee of a job.

Now that employers cannot preclude taking people on if they are not members of a trade union, neither can anyone be prevented from joining a union after being employed, the first question the potential newcomer must ask is whether to go for training and qualifications before seeking a job or whether to opt for the 'on job' apprenticeship route.

## Is training the best route in?

The disadvantage of training, especially if it leads to post graduate courses, is that eventually you will have to look for a job and if you have followed the advice suggested in this book and restricted your search to areas more likely to lead to fulfilling your ultimate ambition, you may find yourself forced to take jobs where your training to begin with is of little use. You may also be in rivalry with people considerably younger than you who may have only recently left school and are therefore better able to work for the low or even no salaries which menial jobs often offer.

Of course, theoretically, those with training should progress faster but this does not take into account the undefinable and untrainable factor of talent which combined with persistence and some luck has been another ongoing theme of this book.

But, on balance, particularly with technical and craft jobs, some form of training is to be advised before seeking a job and, if for any reason, you decide to try to get work without any formal qualifications, make sure you find out about courses that are available once you are employed (see next paragraph).

## FINDING THE RIGHT TRAINING

At last, after many false dawns, one organisation now exists to advise and co-ordinate information about training in broadcast, film and video. Its name is SKILLSET and it was formally launched in 1993; it is funded by the major employers and unions in the industry and is recognised as the sector's voice on training nationally and internationally. It operates at a strategic level within the industry providing relevant labour market and training information, encouraging higher levels of investment in training and implementing occupational standards and the Scottish and National Vocational Qualifications based upon them (see page 165). SKILLSET also publish a very comprehensive *Career Handbook for TV, Radio, Film, Video and Interactive Media*.

For careers advice contact: SKILLSET, Focus Point, 21 Caledonian Road, London N1 9GB. Tel: (020) 7713 9800. Email: *info@skillset.org* Website: *www.skillset.org* and *www.skillsformedia.com*

### Other information about training

Recently, there has been a proliferation of universities offering degrees in cinematics, covering film, television and photography and media studies which can also include communications, journalism and publishing. So, more than ever, it is good to try to look ahead to see where your ultimate ambitions lie. Not that there is anything against switching careers but you might waste a lot of time and money taking a university course that's not right for you.

So how do you make the right choice? SKILLSET (see above) and the British Film Institute have a website *www.bfi.org.uk/ mediacourses* which lists courses available, so check this and talk to SKILLSET as well.

## The UK Film Skills Strategy

From 2004, an ambitious industry and lottery funded scheme for training in all branches of production has come into being, catering for students as well as those with a foot in the door already.

Briefly, this consists of a Course Approval system awarded to training establishments which have the greatest 'career aware-ness' attitude for their graduates. The industry also recognises a limited number of training colleges who adopt the most realistic approach to jobs in production. These are awarded the title 'Screen Academy'.

So when you come to check out the bewildering number of universities and other educational bodies, ask if they have the Course Approval seal of SKILLSET and the UK Film Council. And if they've been given Screen Academy status as well, so much the better!

But however exciting and overdue these developments are, it is doubtful whether there will be any guarantee of a job when you emerge from whatever training you've completed. So the next chapter, Selling Yourself, is probably still the *most important* aspect of fulfilling your ambition to get into films or television.

## Accredited Film Schools

The following film schools were the original ones recognised by

BECTU (Broadcasting Entertainment and Cinematograph Union). They therefore still offer very professional training with possibly the highest proportion of successful students who subsequently get jobs in film or television.

The Media School, Bournemouth University, Weymouth House, Fern Barrow, Talbot Campus, Poole, Dorset BH12 5BB. Tel: (01202) 965360. Website: *www.bournemouth.ac.uk/media*

University of Bristol, Cantocks Close, Woodland Road, Bristol BS8 1UP. Tel: (01179) 545481. Fax: (01173) 315082. Website: *www.bristol.ac.uk/drama*

London College of Communication, Department of Media, Elephant and Castle, London SE1 6SB. Tel: (020) 7514 6859. Website: *www.lcc.arts.ac.uk*

London Film School, 24 Shelton Street, London WC2H 9UB. Tel: (020) 7836 9642. Fax: (020) 7497 3718. Website: *www.lfs.org.uk*

National Film and Television School, Beaconsfield Studios, Station Road, Beaconsfield, Bucks HP9 1LG. Tel: (01494) 671234. Fax: (01494) 674042. Email: *admin@nftsfilm-tv.ac.uk*

Ravensbourne College of Design and Communication, Walden Road, Chislehurst, Kent BR7 5SN. Tel: (020) 8289 4900. Ravensbourne is moving shortly to new premises in Greenwich Peninsula. See their website for particulars: *www.ravensbourne.ac.uk*

University of Westminster, School of Media, Arts and Design, Northwick Park, Harrow, Middlesex HA1 3TP. Tel: (020) 7911 5000. Fax: (020) 7911 5955. Email: *harrow-admissions@westminster.ac.uk*

University of Wales, Newport, Department of Media Arts, PO Box 179, Caerleon Campus, Newport NP18 3YG. Tel: (01633) 430088. Fax: (01633) 432610.

The Surrey Institute of Art and Design, University College, Falkner Road, Farnham, Surrey GU9 7DS. Tel: (01252) 722441. Fax: (01252) 892616. Email: *registry@surrart.ac.uk* Website: *http://www.surrart.ac.uk*

## The National Film and Television School

Of the above, undoubtedly the best in Britain, possibly in Europe, is the National Film and Television School. Here is an excerpt from their prospectus:

> The National Film and Television School is the UK's national centre of excellence for postgraduate education in film and TV programme making. Our talented, creative and enthusiastic community of students makes around one hundred films a year, under the guidance of tutors who are leaders in their professional fields – teachers like Stephen Frears (*Dirty Pretty Things*) in Fiction Direction, Brian Tufano (*Trainspotting*) in Cinematography and Nik Powell, our director, and a producer himself (*Calendar Girls, Little Voice, The Crying Game*).
>
> At the NFTS, you'll do real filmmaking in industry standard facilities where working methods model professional practice. Practice and more practice is the key to becoming a film and TV programme maker. From initial concept to post-production, everyone works together as a team and each student graduates with both professional skills in their own field and a good understanding of the other major roles involved in bringing a new film or TV programme to the screen.

The NFTS is unusual among film schools in providing purpose-built film/TV studios and facilities to learn in. Our film and television stage, animation and production design studios, edit suites, sound post-production facilities, music recording studio and dubbing theatre are all furnished with new generation digital equipment equivalent to that used at the highest level in today's film and TV industry.

*Courses offered*
The NFTS offers two-year MA courses in Animation, Cinematography, Composing for Film and TV, Documentary Direction, Editing, Fiction Direction, Producing, Production Design, Screenwriting and Sound Post-production. There is a one-year Diploma in Sound Recording, and a two-year, part-time Script Development Executive Diploma, run in association with the Script Factory. Courses which started in 2005 include Creative Factual TV Producing (2-year Diploma, seeking MA validation) and a 15-month Diploma in Digital Post-Production.

*Entry requirements*
Whether studying for a Diploma or an MA, a degree or other educational qualification is not required – relevant experience counts for more. The NFTS looks for people with talent, commitment, passion and the ability to work collaboratively and who already have some experience or training in their specialist area or a related field – even if it's just making their own DV film. Most students are in their mid-twenties on entry but there is no hard-and-fast rule on age.

For a prospectus, apply to the NFTS (see page 149 for address) or visit the NFTS website at *www.nftsfilm-tv.ac.uk*

## National Short Course Training Programme (nsctp)

The National Short Course Training Programme (nsctp) is the leading training provider of high quality, cost effective short courses to professional standards for the majority of freelancers working in the film and television industry. Courses are aimed at those who have worked in the industry for at least two years, although there are a few courses aimed at those new to film and television.

All nsctp courses are intensely practical, organised in small workshop-style groups and are tutored by some of the best professionals working in the film, television and related media industries.

Short courses (from one day to 15 days) are run throughout the year and cover a wide range of skills in different specialist areas for people at varying levels of experience in:

- cameras and lighting
- sound – location recording and post-production
- editing
- design
- writing and directing
- production – from assistant to producer level
- computer graphics and animation (Flame, Smoke, AfterFX, Shake, Maya, 3DS Max and Combustion).

All courses are linked to Skillset Professional Qualifications (formerly NVQs) where appropriate and supporting paperwork can often be used in a candidate's portfolio of evidence. In addition, all nsctp courses having a legal content have been accredited by the Law Society and the Bar Association for those needing CPD (continuing professional development) credits. The nsctp is also unique in that its courses have been validated at Master's degree level, enabling industry professionals to attain an MA in Film and Television while continuing to work.

For further information, contact the NSCTP. Tel: (01494) 677903. Fax: (01494) 678708. Email: *info@nfts-scu.org.uk* Website: *www.nfts-scu.org.uk*

## COURSES WITH PARTICULAR SPECIALITIES

It would be invidious to attempt to grade the great number of establishments in the UK offering film or video training. You will have to compare their prospectuses, qualifications for entry and location to find the most suitable for you.

There are however some schools which have a reputation for particular areas so some of these are specified here.

### University affiliation

University of Bristol, Arts Faculty Office, 3–5 Woodland Road, Bristol BS8 1TB. Tel: (01179) 287426. *www.bristol.ac.uk/arts*

A one year postgraduate MA/diploma in Film and Television Production which is 70% practical and 30% critical. Unique in that it is affiliated to the University's department of drama.

### Animation

University College for the Creative Arts of Canterbury, Epsom, Farnham, Maidstone and Rochester. The first undergraduate course in the UK to offer a degree in animation. See their website *www.surrart.ac.uk*

Computer Animation (Undergraduate course)
Digital Special Effects, Computer Animation, Digital Entertainment systems (post-graduate)
Bournemouth Media School, Bournemouth University, Talbot
   Campus, Fern Barrow, Poole, Dorset BH12 5BB.
   Tel: (01202) 595371. Fax: (01202) 595099.
   Email: (undergraduate) *macugrad@bournemouth.ac.uk*
   Email: (post-graduate) *macpgrad@bournemouth.ac.uk*

## Good basic training

The London Film Academy opened in 2002 with a very down-to-earth approach. They offer a one-year course in all branches of film production, shooting and editing on film. The theory is that everybody should learn the basics of technique no matter what you might finally work on or in what area – a very good philosophy! For more information contact: The London Film Academy, The Old Church, 52A Walham Grove, London SW6 1QR. Tel: (020) 7386 7711. Website: *www.londonfilmacademy.co.uk*

## Electricians

A one year full time or two year part time City and Guilds 181 Entertainments and Theatre Electricians course is operated by the Faculty of Visual and Performing Arts of the City of Westminster College. It covers a wide range of relevant subjects such as Electrical Principles, Craft Theory, Performance Lighting, Electrical Workshops, Practical Assignments and Computer Applications.

This course originally came about as a result of an initiative between the College, The Moving Image Society (formerly BKSTS, British Kinematograph Sound and Television Society) and leading lighting contractors and programme makers led by Samuelson Lighting Ltd.

For further particulars contact: Faculty of Visual and Performing Arts, Info-Point, City of Westminster College, 25 Paddington Green, London W2 1NB. Tel: (020) 7723 8826. Fax: (020) 7258 2700. Email: *www.cwc.ac.uk*

## Training in make-up and hair

Greasepaint run a course in make-up, hair and prosthetics (modelling of the face in plastics, etc). Contact: Greasepaint Ltd, 143 Northfield Avenue, London W13 9QT. Tel: (020) 8840 6000. Email: *info@greasepaint.co.uk* Website: *www.greasepaint.co.uk*

Brushstroke operate from Shepperton Studios and have 3, 4 and 9 month courses in Make-Up, Hair and High Fashion Make-Up. Contact: Brushstroke, Shepperton Film Studios, Studio Road, Shepperton, Middlesex TW17 0QP. Tel: 01932 592463. Email: *info@brushstroke.co.uk*
Website: *www.brushstroke.co.uk*

## Short courses

For those who enter the film and television industries without any formal training from film schools, there are now a number of short courses to enable people to improve their skills in production and creative jobs and get up to date with new equipment and techniques.

They are all fee paying, so you will have to find out whether your employer is prepared to pay for you.

The majority of short courses however relate to work in video and audio recording and editing because it is here that the technology and equipment tend to change most. As the dates and duration of each course are different each year, it is best if you contact the following organisations to find out their programmes, but although they may accept people not already working in the industries, they are broadly intended for employed people to improve their qualifications, however humble their job may be at present.

1.  Short Course Unit, Ravensbourne College, School of Broadcasting, Walden Road, Chislehurst, Kent BR7 5SN. Tel: (020) 8289 4900. email: *short.courses@rave.ac.uk*

2.  VET Ltd, The Lux Building, 2–4 Hoxton Square, London N1 6US. Tel: (020) 7505 4700. Fax: (020) 7505 4800. Email: *training@vet.co.uk* Website: *www.vet.co.uk*

3.  The National Short Course Training Programme, The National Film and Television School, Beaconsfield Studios, Station Road, Beaconsfield, Bucks HP9 1LG. Tel: (01494) 677903.

# FT2

This stands for **Film and Television Freelance Training** – the only UK wide provider of new entrant training for junior construction, production and technical grades for the freelance sector of the industry which is both industry funded and managed.

The **New Entrant Technical Training Programme** is a two year, full time, training programme for young people wishing to enter the industry as junior production and technical grade assistants. Apprenticeship in style, training is delivered through a sequence of production attachments across features, television drama, documentaries, commercials, corporates and promos and specially commissioned short course training delivered by recognised industry centres of excellence. All trainees work towards achievement of the Skillset NVQs at Levels 2 and 3 relevant to their grade.

Whilst on the programme, trainees receive a monthly training allowance and financial assistance with travel, child and dependent care costs where appropriate.

## Areas in which training is offered

Camera Assistant/Clapper Loader, Assistant Editor, Art Department Assistant, Production Assistant, Assistant Script Supervisor, or Production Co-ordinator, Grip, Make-up/Hair Assistant, Props Assistant, Sound Assistant and Wardrobe Assistant. Researchers for factual programmes can apply to go on an 18 month course run by the Independent Researcher Training Scheme.

FT2 does *not* train Directors, Producers or Scriptwriters.

## Selection

For training as a Make-up/Hair Assistant you must have achieved both NVQs in Hairdressing and Beauty Therapy at Level 2 (or equivalent) and if you wish to train in Production you must have achieved the NVQ in Administration at Level 2, possess excellent word processing skills and a proven touch typing speed of 40wpm and an administration or secretarial qualification.

For these and the other areas, applicants must have demonstrable commitment and enthusiasm for film and television, a strong visual sense, highly developed communication and interpersonal skills and the determination and tenacity to succeed in the freelance labour market. The scheme is funded by the Skillset Freelance Training Fund and the European Social Fund and standard ESF Eligibility Criteria apply.

## Application

All applications on the official FT2 Application form are considered (the closing date for applications is normally the 1st April of each year) and those that are successful at this stage are invited to an interview where their suitability for and understanding of the scheme are considered. The panel is composed of practitioners and recent graduates from the scheme. Offers of places are made starting usually in the late Summer.

Competition is fierce with usually between 40 to 60 applicants for each available place, so once more it is up to you to sell yourself as hard as possible.

Recruitment usually opens in February of each year and application forms and further background information on the scheme are downloadable from the website or by sending an A4 sae stating which position you are applying for.

## Setcrafts Apprenticeship Training Scheme

In 1996, FT2, with financial support from Skillset, launched the Setcrafts Apprenticeship Training Scheme which recruited six young people seeking to establish careers as freelance carpenters, fibrous plasterers and set painters in features and commercials.

The Apprentices receive a monthly salary and are attached to a sequence of features and commercials as members of crew and undertake four week blocks of formal training at industry recognised centres of crafts training excellence acquiring the skills and knowledge to achieve the relevant grade NVQ at Level 3.

For information on FT2 and the above schemes (including entry requirements) visit FT2's website at *www.ft2.org.uk* Or write enclosing an A4 sae to: FT2 – Film and Television Freelance Training, Third Floor, 18–20 Southwark Street, London SE1 1TJ. Tel: (020) 7407 0344. Fax: (020) 7407 0366.
Email: *info@ft.2org.uk* Website: *www.ft2.org*

## WORKING FOR THE **BBC**

Of all the training for jobs both creative and technical in film and television, the BBC's is the oldest established and the most comprehensive.

Previously only for those accepted for employment, the BBC's Training and Development Centre at Wood Norton, Worcs, at Elstree and at Marylebone, London are open to anyone who can pay. Tel: 0870 1220216. Fax: 0870 1220145.
Email: *training@bbc.co.uk* Website: *www.bbctraining.co.uk*

In the UK, the BBC is still the largest employer in television and its charter decrees that all vacancies open to external candidates have to be publicly advertised in national or local papers and trade publications with a summary on Ceefax page 996.

But what this also means is that the applications for jobs in nearly all areas greatly outnumber the vacancies available. And with the increasing sub-contracting of programme production to independent companies, recruitment has changed, resulting in more short-term contracts.

## Information

They publish full information about working in the BBC, the qualifications required, training provided and how to apply for vacancies.

So the first step if you want to work for the BBC is to study these in your chosen area, remembering that, in addition to the educational qualifications and any technical experience you may have, you must convince anyone you write to or see of your keenness and dedication.

The BBC is an equal opportunities employer and positively welcomes applications from under-represented groups. The BBC is also trying to encourage more flexible work patterns, job sharing and flexi-time for example.

## Where to apply for the BBC

For further general information about working for the BBC, try the BBC interactive telephone Careers Information Service, *Voices*, on (020) 8576 0639 or use the BBC World of Opportunity website at *www.jobs.bbc.co.uk* Finally, you can subscribe to the BBC staff magazine *Ariel*, PO Box 324, Griffin House, Aylesbury, Bucks HP19 3BP, where vacancies are advertised.

When applying for jobs which you have seen advertised, you may have to contact the particular department concerned but this will be indicated in the advertisement.

## BBC ENGINEERING AND TECHNICAL OPERATIONS (BROADCAST TECHNOLOGY)

The BBC has an international reputation for the quality of its programmes and much of this is due to its long standing commitment to maintaining and improving engineering and technical standards.

What are the various jobs and who are the people who operate and maintain the complex equipment used in television?

### Engineers

These are the people who maintain studio equipment, such as vision mixers, camera channels and sound desks to ensure that the facilities are fully available for the programme makers.

They may be involved in the engineering aspects of video tape recording and film replay equipment. Engineers may also work with film equipment, with outside broadcasts and news and current affairs which include the co-ordination of satellite links and live inserts in news programmes.

Virtually all these different areas can be found in the BBC regions as well as in London.

### Qualifications for entry

To join as a trainee engineer, you must be at least 18 and you'll need GCSE grade A-C in English, Maths and Physics, and Maths and Physics to A level as well; an ordinary BTEC diploma in Electrical/Electronic Engineering will be considered as an alternative to A levels.

To join as a graduate engineer you require a degree in electrical or electronic engineering.

There is also a scheme for graduates in disciplines other than electronics who want to transfer to this field. There are other areas like Engineering Research and Design which employ engineers. Degree sponsorship and industrial training may also be available.

## Technical Operators

These are the people who actually operate the television cameras, the sound equipment and film replay and videotape recording equipment.

As with engineers, they may work in London or the Regions and on the whole range of programmes.

Again, you must be at least 18 to start as a trainee and have normal hearing and colour vision.

A good standard of education is required, for example GCSE grade A–C (or the equivalent) in English, Maths and Physics but just as importantly, you must demonstrate a good general understanding of the area that interests you and a practical interest in associated topics such as hi-fi sound, tape recording, photography or music.

## Sponsorship

The BBC now offers sponsorship, pre-university, industrial and vacation training for those people keen to develop a career in electronic engineering, project engineering or practical operational engineering. Sponsorship is usually for a maximum of three years and is for degree-level students in electronic engineering or similar. One-year pre-university training which may lead to subsequent sponsorship is also available in some departments. Vacation training provides six weeks during the summer for students to gain practical work experience in the BBC. For further particulars contact: Careers Information Service *Voices*. Tel: (020) 8576 0639 or BBC World of Opportunity website at *www.bbctraining.com*

## ITV AND INDEPENDENT COMPANIES

Training in ITV and independent companies is not as formalised as in the BBC for the simple reason that they operate in different parts of the country and are all different in size and complexity.

Many ITV companies do, however, run new entrant schemes. For example, Yorkshire TV takes a few people on a two-year graduate scheme and others take a very few on year-long placements. Some offer the chance to go on courses at colleges like Ravensbourne.

## Ravensbourne College of Design and Communication

Ravensbourne College of Design and Communication is a National Centre of Excellence for Broadcasting. It offers a range of courses within the field of broadcasting at both further and higher education level.

The degree and foundation degree courses are as follows: an accelerated two-year BA (Hons) Content Creation and New Media; a two-year Foundation Degree (Arts) Broadcast Operations and Production; a two-year Foundation Degree (Arts)

Broadcast Post Production; a two-year Foundation Degree (Science) Broadcast Media Technology, a two-year Foundation Degree (Arts) Creative Sound Design and a two-year Foundation Degree (Arts) Computer Visualisation and Animation. The five latter courses also feature an optional one-year top-up to turn them into full BA (Hons) Degrees, as with all the courses except the Broadcast Media Technology which will become a BSc (Hons).

Broadcasting is housed in a £5.6 million complex built in 1991 using advanced digital equipment as well as analogue. All practical work is carried out to broadcast standards.

It is also possible for full time students to obtain relevant attachments with a television or facilities company. Ravensbourne provides a very sound grounding for anyone interested in getting into television in any broad production, technical or engineering job. The fact that over the last few years 93% of their students have obtained employment speaks for itself.

For further particulars apply to: Ravensbourne College of Design and Communication, Walden Road, Chislehurst, Kent BR7 5SN. Tel: (020) 8289 4900. Fax: (020) 8325 8320. Email: *info@rave.ac.uk* Website: *rave.ac.uk*

## WORKSHOPS

Workshops are small production units which work on a non-profit distributing basis. They may also be involved in distribution, education and exhibition of films and videos.

They generally undertake work of a radical nature addressed to particular audiences such as the young, women or black people.

Although not strictly acting as training grounds for technicians, people who have a particular interest in this type of work could look out for lowly jobs in the hope of getting more closely involved in actual production at a later date.

By taking advantage of further training on a short course for example this could be one very commendable route to take.

You can find a list of workshops in the *British Film Institute Film and Television Handbook* (see Appendix).

## NATIONALLY RECOGNISED QUALIFICATIONS FOR FILM AND TV

Apart from graduation from film school and the qualifications which apply to engineering and some technical jobs, actual proof of experience and competence, apart from a list of credits of productions on which you have worked, has never been possible to obtain by film and television technicians.

This has changed over recent years with the development of National Occupational Standards and qualifications based on them called National and Scottish Vocational Qualifications. These NVQs/SVQs (called SKILLSET Professional Qualifications) have been drawn up for broadcast, film, video and interactive media by SKILLSET – the Sector Skills Council for the industry. There are standards for almost all occupations and qualifications for various levels in areas where it is appropriate or there is a demand. The qualifications are fast becoming the currency in parts of the industry. This enables employers to recognise competence, and individuals to prove they can do the jobs. Work is on-going to develop standards for producers and directors, and following completion of this work it will be decided whether it is appropriate to then also develop qualifications for these occupations. Any such qualifications will have to recognise the competencies of talent and entrepreneurial skills in their assessment. Occupational standards are available on the SKILLSET website which is useful for planning your career.

For further information contact: SKILLSET, Focus oint, 21 Caledonian Road, London N1 9GB. Tel: (020) 7713 9800. Fax: (020) 7713 9801. Email: *info@skillset.org* Website: *www.skillset.org www.skillsformedia.com*

## Training in Scotland and Wales

**Scottish Screen Training** is an employer-led partnership and provides training based on the current needs of the industry. For further information contact: Scottish Screen Training, 249 West George Street, Glasgow G2 4QE. Tel: 0845 300 7300. Email: *info@scottishscreen.com*

**CYFLE** runs a twelve-month full-time course and a number of short courses with particular emphasis on Welsh-speaking technicians. For further information contact: CYFLE, 33–35 West Bute Street, Cardiff CF10 5LH. Tel: (02920) 465533. Email: *cyfle@cyfle.co.uk* Website: *www.cyfle.co.uk*

## INTRODUCTORY COURSE

There is a good introductory course in London with sessions at weekends giving an overview of all aspects of production. Run by professionals in the indusry and excellent for people who want a taste of the business but are not sure what area to go for.

Contact: Panico, PO Box 496, London WC1A 2WZ. Tel: (020) 7485 3533. Email: *panico@panicofilms.com* Website: *www.panicofilms.com*

### *Draft Zero*

Short courses for development executives and screenwriters. Information about Draft Zero from The Film Commission, Screen South, Pinewood Studios, Iver Heath, Bucks SL0 0NH. Tel: (01753) 656 412.
Email: *draftzero.com*. Website: *www.draftzero.com*

### *Websites with job opportunities*

Largely vacancies for experienced people but occasional openings for runners.
*www.editors@produxion.com*
*www.mandy.com*
*www.shootingpeople.org*
*www.productionbase.co.uk*
*www.broadcastfreelancers.com*

## SUMMING UP

Training courses, apprenticeships and vacancies change so rapidly nowadays that it is always best to visit organisation websites first to check their latest contact details and particulars.

# 8

# Selling Yourself to Film and Television

It is to be hoped that the previous chapters will have given you some idea of the extent of the various branches of film and television and something about the various jobs in different departments and the possible starting points.

Of course, it is possible to cross from one area of production to another, from one department to another, from film to video and vice-versa but where you start often influences the route you are going to follow throughout your career leading, hopefully, to fulfilling your ultimate ambition.

Remember the magic wand trick suggested in the introduction, and propel yourself forward ten years and see what you would really like to be doing. By this means you can select the most suitable route that leads to this goal.

So now let us turn to what is probably the most important part of this book – selling yourself.

Nearly every job in every area of film and television is highly sought after. For example, when the BBC advertise a vacancy for a film trainee they get hundreds of applicants. So the first thing to remember is that even if you have the best qualifications from the best film and TV school in the world, you still have to convince people of your particular talent and enthusiasm that backs up those qualifications.

And the same applies if you have been somewhat of an educational dropout but feel deep down that you have that elusive talent, persistence and flair to persuade people to give you a chance in favour of everyone else on the same quest.

All this takes time – resign yourself to at least six months for job hunting. Energy – to mount and follow through your own personal sales campaign. And money – for writing letters, sending emails, for telephones, for transport and even buying a sympathetic listener a drink or two.

## A PLAN OF ACTION

So take a leaf out of any organisation that is running a direct mail campaign and emulate them. Here is a list of suggestions to help you sell yourself:

### The right letter

Compose your standard letter carefully but be prepared to modify it according to the addressee if necessary. Word it in as personal terms as you can, giving your reasons for wanting to work in any particular area. Give your technical experience and ask if the person to whom you are writing can spare time to see you and give you advice.

### The right kind of request

DO NOT ASK STRAIGHT OUT FOR A JOB. The chance of your letter arriving at the precise moment that there is a vacancy is fairly slim, unless you have done your research very thoroughly as suggested in Chapter 2 on Feature Films, and you are there just when a production is being crewed up.

■  It is better to ask for a meeting and then seek advice and suggestions as to other people you might contact.

By this means you will build up an expanding file which may lead you in directions you had overlooked.

## The right name

Try to get the name of someone in any organisation, be they producer, production manager or head of the particular department you are aiming for and write to or email them. This does not apply to the BBC where virtually all recruitment is handled on a more formal basis (see Chapter 7 on Training, the BBC). Similarly, ITV companies tend to channel applications through their personnel departments, although it does not do any harm to try to approach individuals in the same way as with independent companies.

## The right personal touch

Attach a formal CV which gives all the facts about you in the normal way, but try to make your accompanying letter look as if it has been written or typed to the person you are addressing. In other words, use the very best method of copying with the addressee's name in the same type style and matching the print density. Everyone knows that you are sending out many letters but no-one likes to be blatantly reminded.

## The right size of mailshot

Send out at least 200 letters or emails but you'll be lucky if you get much response, so follow this up with a call asking to see somebody for advice. Do not push too hard if people are in the middle of a production. In this case, try asking on the telephone for suggestions of other people you might contact. Ask permission to mention to others the name of the person to whom you are talking.

## The right follow up

Keep a careful file with notes of responses, rejections, advice given at interviews and be prepared to make second approaches after a time. If, when you go for an interview, you can make contact with comparative newcomers of a similar age to yourself, try to seek their advice too.

All this requires quite a degree of organisation on your part. But as most work in film and television is freelance, some business knowledge is very useful as you will be expected to invoice for your services after each job, pay or charge VAT, pay tax probably on Schedule D and so on. Here membership of the Trade Union BECTU is a help as they can advise you on all this as well as things like law and insurance. Membership of BECTU can also be good for networking, as is membership of other professional organisations like BAFTA, although three years' experience in film or TV is required before you can become a BAFTA member.

There are several websites you could try for that first break: *www.shootingpeople.org* and *www.mandy.com* are two good ones. They even advertise no or low paid jobs but watch out for shark infested waters! Here the union is trying to introduce a kind of seal of approval to be awarded to genuine low budget ventures. You could also subscribe to websites like *www.productionbase. co.uk* to get yourself known in parallel with your direct mail campaign.

## Saying 'yes'!

Finally, however talented, knowledgeable and well trained you may be, accept any job, however menial, if it is in the area or even adjacent to that which interests you most. Jobs like runners for instance are extremely hard work, often underpaid and may demand little skill but they give to those with ambition the chance to observe the work of experienced technicians, to make contacts and generally get the feel of working in the industry. Do not be too impatient to progress. No employer likes it if you are obviously making your job too transient.

## A FINAL WORD

There is not as much glamour working in films and television as many outside believe; but there is a tremendous amount of hard work, often dedication and even obsession.

Obtaining your first break is a matter of persistence, flair and talent but there is also an element of luck in being there just at the right time and place.

And so to the readers of this book, some of whom hopefully will become the future doyens of film and television, go the best wishes of those who work in these exciting industries and who could not possibly have followed any other careers.

# Appendix of Further Information

## FURTHER READING

### Film and television directories

1. *Animation Directory*, Imagine – The place for animation professionals. *www.imagineanimation.net*

2. *The Creative Handbook*, *www.chb.com*

3. *The BFI Film and Television Handbook*, Published by the British Film Institute, 21 Stephen Street, London W1P 1PL. Tel: (020) 7255 1444. *www.bfi.org.uk*

4. *Kays UK Production Manual*, Published by Kays Media, Pinewood Studios, Pinewood Road, Iver Heath, Bucks SL0 0NH. Tel: (020) 8960 6900 or (01753) 651700. *www.kays.co.uk*

5. *Kemps International Film TV and Video Yearbook*, Read Business Information. *www.kftv.com*

6. *The Knowledge*, Hollis Publishing. *www.theknowledgeonline.com*

7. *Screen International Film & TV Directory*, Emap Publishing *www.screeninternational.com*

### Trade journals

1. *Audio Visual* (Monthly)
2. *Broadcast* (Weekly)

3. *Campaign* (Weekly)
4. *Creation* (Monthly)
5. *Hollywood Reporter International* (Weekly)
6. *Marketing Week* (Weekly)
7. *Media Week* (Weekly)
8. *Moving Pictures International* (Weekly)
9. *Screen International* (Weekly)
10. *Stage and Television Today* (Weekly)
11. *Televisual* (Monthly)
12. *Variety* (Weekly)

## General publications

1. *Careers in Film and Video* Kogan Page: R. Ostrov and B. McCoid

2. *Careers in Independent Television* ITV Association: Sue Davis

3. *Careers in TV and Radio* Kogan Page: J. Allen

4. *Film and TV – The Way In* British Film Institute: Robert Angell

5. *Getting Jobs in Broadcasting* Cassell: Fiona Russell

6. *Lights, Camera, Action* British Film Institute: Josephine Langham

7. *Careers leaflets* Royal Television Society

8. *A Woman's Guide to Jobs in Film & Television* Pandora: Anne Ross Muir

9. *Media Studies UK*, British Film Institute

10. *Information Pack*, Skillset, Prospect House, 80–110 New Oxford Street, London WC1A 1HB.

11. *Media Guide*, Edited by Steve Peak, published by *The Guardian*

12. *Television Researchers' Guide* BBC Publications: Kathy Chater

13. *Career Handbook for TV, Radio, Film, Video and Interactive Media*. Published by Skillset (see 10 above)

14. *The Scriptwriter*, 2 Elliott House, London NW3 3SU. Tel: (020) 7586 4853 *www.scriptwritermagazine.com*

15. *How to get a job in television*, Susan Walls, How To Books

## Useful addresses

1. Advertising Film and Videotape Producers Association (AFVPA), 26 Noel Street, London W1V 3RD.

2. British Academy of Film & Television Arts (BAFTA), 195 Piccadilly, London W1J 9LN.

3. BBC Careers Information Service, Voices (020) 8576 0639.

4. BBC Recruitment Services, Engineering (020) 8675 0639.

5. British Film Institute, 21 Stephen Street, London W1P 1PL.

6. The Cinema Bookshop, 13 Great Russell Street, London WC1B 3NH.

7. Independent Television Association (ITVA), Knighton House, 56 Mortimer Street, London W1N 8AN.

8. International Visual Communications Association (IVCA), Bolsover House, 5/6 Clipstone Street, London W1P 7EB.

9. FT2, Warwick House, 9 Warwick Street, London W1B 5LY.

10. Kodak Ltd, Motion Picture and Television Division, Kodak House, PO Box 66, Hemel Hempstead, Herts HP1 1JU.

11. BKSTS – The Moving Image Society, 5 Walpole Court, Ealing Studios, Ealing Green, London W5 5ED.

12. New Producers Alliance, 9 Boulet Close, London W1W 7BP.

13. PCR and Filmlog, PO Box 100, Ramsgate, Kent CT11 7DA.

14. PACT (Producers Alliance for Cinema and Television), 45 Mortimer Street, London W1N 7RD.

15. Royal Television Society, 5th Floor, Kildare House, 3 Dorset Rise, London EC4Y 8EN.

16. Writers' Guild of Great Britain, 40 Rosebury Avenue, London EC1R 4RX.

17. Zwemmers Bookshop, 80 Charing Cross Road, London WC2H 0BB.

18. Offstage Theatre and Film Bookshop, 37 Chalk Farm Road, London NW1 8AJ.

## Trade Unions

1. BECTU (Broadcasting, Entertainment, Cinematograph and Theatre Union), 373–377 Clapham Road, London SW9 9BT.

## PRINCIPAL BROADCASTING ORGANISATIONS IN THE UK

1. BBC Television, Television Centre, Wood Lane, London W12 7RJ. Tel: (020) 8743 8000.

2. Anglia Television, Anglia House, Norwich NR1 3JG. Tel: (01603) 615151.

3. Border Television, The Television Centre, Carlisle CA1 3NT. Tel: (01228) 25101.

4. Central Independent Television, Central House, Broad Street, Birmingham B1 2JP. Tel: (0121) 643 9898.

5. Channel Four Television, 124 Horseferry Road, London SW1P 2TX. Tel: (020) 7396 4444.

6. Channel Television, The Television Centre, St Helier, Jersey, Channel Islands. Tel: (01534) 73999.

7. GMTV, London Television Centre, Upper Ground, London SE1 0LT. Tel: (020) 7827 7000.

8. Grampian Television, Queens Cross, Aberdeen AB9 2XJ. Tel: (01224) 646464.

9. HTV Wales, The Television Centre, Cathedral Road, Cardiff CF1 9XL. Tel: (01222) 590590.

10. Independent Television News, 200 Grays Inn Road, London WC1X 8XZ. Tel: (020) 7833 3000.

11. ITV plc, ITV Network Centre, 200 Grays Inn Road, London WC1X 8HF. Tel: (020) 7843 8000.

12. London Weekend Television, South Bank Television Centre, Kent House, Upper Ground, London SE1 9LT. Tel: (020) 7620 1620.

13. Meridian Broadcasting, Television Centre, Northam, Southampton, Hants SO9 5H2. Tel: (01703) 222555.

14. Scottish Television, Cowcaddens, Glasgow G2 3PR. Tel: (0141) 332 9999.

15. Tyne Tees Television, The Television Centre, City Road, Newcastle-upon-Tyne NE1 2AL. Tel: (0191) 261 0181.

16. Ulster Television, Havelock House, Ormeau Road, Belfast BT7 1EB. Tel: (01232) 221822.

17. Westcountry Television, Western Wood Way, Langage Science Park, Plymouth, Devon PL7 5BG. Tel: (01752) 333333.

18. Yorkshire Television, The Television Centre, Leeds LS3 1JS. Tel: (0113) 243 82837.

19. TV Sianel Pedwar Cymru (S4C), Parc ty Glas, Llanishen, Cardiff CF4 5DV. Tel: (029) 2074 7444.

*Note*

Independent production companies who may provide programmes and make a wide variety of productions for different outlets are too numerous to list here but the reader is reminded again to refer to the various directories listed in the Appendix. The companies may indicate the area of production in which they specialise. It is suggested you check on Google and their websites for the latest information about all organisations mentioned in this book.

## Sample pages for NVQ in Sound Operations level 3

### Unit S14 – Optimise sound pick up with a handheld microphone

*You ...*

- identify where the microphone is to be positioned
- deal with problems in positioning the microphone safely and effectively
- make sure that the microphone position discriminates against unwanted sound sources and noise
- position the microphone and cable so that they are safe, unobtrusive and will cause the minimum disruption to performance
- capture sound with the perspective, dynamic range and stereo information required
- achieve an appropriate balance between sound sources
- respond to cues immediately and in a well co-ordinated way
- move the microphone smoothly, fluidly and unobtrusively, minimising unwanted sound
- maintain stable stereo images when moving the microphone, when the pick-up is in stereo
- make the microphone secure and safe when not in use.

*Elements*

S14.1  Position the handheld microphone to optimise sound pick up.

S14.2  Move the handheld microphone in response to cues.

## Unit S15 – Create, obtain and select supplementary sound material

*You . . .*

- find out what materials are needed
- get the required material and assess its suitability
- create material when this is required
- offer options to production
- note and label material you create or obtain
- check that the material you have selected is acceptable to production
- check that the content and duration of the material meets requirements
- playback, mix and monitor appropriately in terms of the technical requirement for the material
- judge what is needed to meet artistic requirements (length, content, quality and creative effect)
- make sure that copyright clearances have been obtained
- document and label material you use accurately.

*Elements*

S15.1  Create and obtain supplementary sound material.

S15.2  Select supplementary sound material.

## Unit S16 – Transfer recorded sound to optical film

*You . . .*

- keep the film magazine free from dust, dirt and unwanted

light
- check that all the equipment you use to transfer sound is clean, safe and working properly
- carry out tests to ensure that the transfer process will proceed without fault
- interpret test results accurately, and deal with any faults or other problems
- make sure that exposure settings optimise density in line with cross modulation test, and that the recording machine runs stably
- monitor reproduced material and the optical recorder to make sure there are no transfer faults
- check that each roll of film has the appropriate end cross modulation and flood tests
- protect recorded film from exposure to light
- check the quality of recorded sound.

*Elements*

S16.1   Prepare equipment for transfer.

S16.2   Transfer recorded material.

# Training and Working Overseas

As stated in the Preface, this book, when originally written, was addressed primarily to readers who wanted to work and train in the United Kingdom. But the growth in production both national and international all over the world can only lead to more opportunities in training and employment wherever you live. So if you are interested in finding training outside the UK, contact **CILECT** (Centre International de Liaison Ecoles de Cinéma et de Télévision) which is an association of film schools and other educational establishments in virtually every country in the world. Contact the Executive Secretary of CILECT, Rue Thérésienne 8, 1000 Bruxelles, Belgium. Tel: +32(0) 476 348 126. Fax: +32(0) 2511 9839. Email: *henry.verhasselt@cilect.org* Website: *www.cilect.org*

For those who want to immerse themselves in an intense way in an international film atmosphere with a chance to meet people of influence from many different countries, a course at **The European Film College** based at Carl Th. Dreyers Veg 1, 8400 Ebeltoft, Denmark Tel: +45 8634 0055; Fax: +45 8634 0535, email: *administration@efc.dk* Website: *www.efc.dk* could be rewarding. But you will need access to funds: a nine-month course costs nearly £6,000 sterling, including all accommodation and tuition. The college stresses this is *not* a film school, rather a form of very high-powered media studies which provides thought-provoking discussion with students and lecturers as well as very useful contacts and advice as to where your future career might lead. That is not to say that there is no involvement in production – the college owns eight Sony Hi-8 cameras and has three editing suites. Moreover, students are encouraged to form study groups to carry out their own projects. But all this is no substitute for a course at a recognised film school.

For over eighty years, the United States has dominated film production and distribution throughout the world and it is true to say that no other industry has been so powerful for so long. California, and Hollywood in particular, has been traditionally the centre for production of feature films whilst the East Coast and New York were originally the hub of television activity. But in spite of less emphasis on continuous major studio production schedules and the growth of location shooting, Hollywood continues to be the acknowledged centre of the film industry, housing the headquarters of the big league players although their interests now embrace other forms of media and production for television is a major activity in the studios.

It is natural therefore that of the many educational establishments throughout the United States, those in California have acquired enviable reputations for excellence. One of the best known is **University of Los Angeles (UCLA)**. Here the **School of Theater, Film and Television** in the words of the Dean, Gilbert Cates, 'offers an intensive discipline-based curriculum which recognises the inherent differences of theater, film and television, affirms their similarities and encourages their interaction.'

The Department includes both production and critical studies programs, with approximately 265 graduate and 60 undergraduate students. The 50 faculty members include leading scholars as well as members of the Los Angeles and international film and television professional communities. In production, graduate specialisations are offered in film and television production, screenwriting, animation and the producers' program. The critical studies program offers MA and PhD degrees for the advanced scholarly study of film and television. Resources include three sound stages, three television studios, extensive editing, scoring and viewing facilities and a complete animation laboratory for both traditional and computer-generated animation.

There are a few places gained each year by students outside the United States under the Education Abroad program but, as in all major film schools throughout the world, competition for all places is extremely tough. But with UCLA's location and with former students like Francis Ford Coppola, Allison Anders, Rob Reiner and Tim Robbins, the School has a reputation to be greatly admired.

Applications should be made by November for admission in the following year Fall Quarter. For more detailed information apply to UCLA, School of Theater, Film and Television, Box 951622, Los Angeles, CA90095-1622, USA. Fax: (310) 825 8787 (310) 825 3383. Website: *www.tft.ucla.edu/info.cfm*

**The University of Southern California School of Cinema-Television** offers professional and academic degrees at bachelors, masters and doctoral levels. Bachelor of Arts students can choose either a Film/Video Production or Critical Studies track.

Bachelor of Fine Arts – Filmic Writing is for students who wish to receive intensive training for non-fiction and fiction screen-writing. Master of Arts, Cinema-Television allows a track in either Film/Video Production or Critical Studies. Master of Fine Arts, Cinema-Television offers a professional degree in two tracks: Film/Video Production and Screenwriting. In addition, the school offers Master of Fine Arts, Film, Video and Computer Animation; Master of Fine Arts – Motion Picture Producing; Doctor of Philosophy, Cinema-Television Critical Studies; Doctor of Philosophy, Cinema-Television Film, Literature and Culture and finally, Cinema-Television Minor which enables a student to learn the basic elements of motion pictures and film studies whilst majoring in another field. *But* students who enter this program cannot subsequently apply for admission to any Cinema-Television major.

USC is a private institution which does not receive direct subsidies from governmental agencies. The School of Cinema-Television depends principally on tuition income and the proceeds of modest endowments and generous gifts from its friends and alumni. Tuition costs are comparable to those at other distinguished private institutions in the United States.

There are some scholarships that are available for under-graduates and graduates. For example: Eastman Kodak Scholarship, John Huston Scholarship, William Morris Agency, Jack Nicholson Scholarships, Mary Pickford Foundation Awards and George Cukor Award. These illustrious names serve as reminders of the proximity of USC to Hollywood and of the interest taken by professionals in the progress of students of The University of South California School of Cinema-Television.

Applications for admission should be made by 1 February for the following Fall semester and 1 November for the following Spring semester. For further information contact: Cinema-Television Office of Student Affairs or USC Office of Undergraduate Admission, University Park, Los Angeles, CA 90089-0911, USA. Tel: (213) 740 2311. Email: *admissions@cinema.usc.edu*. Website: *www.usc.edu*

## AND FINALLY...

A final reminder to all readers of this book, wherever you live and wherever you would like to work in whatever capacity. **Jobs in production anywhere in the world are highly competitive and the number of applicants is usually enormous for every single vacancy**.

It is therefore up to you, whether by training or willingness to learn, to persuade any potential employer that *you* are the right person for the job. All this requires time, persistence, building up your contacts and even a modicum of luck!

But stay with it, so that you can join those of us who have devoted our lives to production in film and television and who could not possibly have followed any other career.

# Glossary

**ADR (Automatic dialogue replacement).** The recording in a studio of dialogue of which the original recording is unsuitable.

**Animatic.** A trial commercial perhaps filmed from the storyboard and with a rough sound track.

**Call sheet.** Full instructions for next day's filming.

**Cutting copy.** The assembly in script order of prints of picture and sound.

**Distributor.** An individual or company that acts for the producer as wholesaler, arranging outlets in cinemas, on television or video and DVD for a film or programme.

**Dolly.** Trolley for moving a camera during a shot. May be on a smooth surface or on specially laid tracks – hence tracking shot. More elaborate devices are called jibs, velocilators and cranes.

**Dubbing.** The mixing of various film sound tracks – dialogue, music and sound effects at the correct levels. The term can also be used for matching dialogue in a language other than the one in which it was originally recorded.

**ENG (Electronic news gathering).** Portable professional video cameras.

**Exhibitor.** Owner and/or operator of a cinema.

**FT2.** Film and Television Freelance Training.

**FX.** Slang term for sound effects.

**The floor.** 'On the floor' is the term used for shooting in a studio as opposed to an exterior location but may be loosely used for working on the production crew of a film.

**Floor manager.** The chief organisational person in a television studio, the equivalent of a first assistant director in film.

**Four waller.** A studio that is available for hire with the barest minimum, if any, facilities provided other than the building.

**Gaffer.** A chief electrician.

**Gallery.** The control rooms – engineering, cameras, sound and direction – of a television production using multi-camera technique. For OBs these are housed in a vehicle called a colour mobile control room or scanner.

**Grading.** Making correct colour rendition of each scene in a film.

**Grip.** The person responsible for whatever device is used for moving a film camera during a shot. Also responsible for transporting camera equipment.

**'Harry'.** Sophisticated electronic animation equipment which can also combine with live action, graphics and paintbox to produce an enormous variety of visual effects on video.

**'Indie'.** Independent production company as opposed to ITV, Independent Television companies who have the franchise to provide programmes for the UK commercial network.

**Non-theatrical release.** Showings to non-paying audiences, usually via libraries to schools, universities or specialist groups.

**Off-line edit.** The first rough video edit on low band, that is non broadcast quality videotape or DVD.

**On-line edit.** The final edit incorporating titles, visual effects and sound track on to the highest quality master tape, dependent on the budget and ultimate release of the programme.

**Optical.** Fades in/out, dissolves, mixes or any other visual effect for transition from one scene to another that is not a straight cut. Less popular in film now but used extensively in pop videos, titles and so on.

**Reader**. Somebody employed by a film or television production company to sift through ideas and scripts submitted and assess and report on their suitability for production.

**Rostrum camera**. Camera mounted on a rock steady base, usually vertically, used in animation. A rostrum can also be used as a term in a studio or on location for building a steady platform for a camera or lights.

**Rushes (US dailies)**. Film and sound used during the day, processed overnight and viewed as soon as possible the following day.

**Seed money (Development finance)**. Initial finance for any film or TV project to enable a script to be commissioned and preliminary work and costing to be carried out.

**Set-up**. What is actually seen through the viewfinder of a camera.

**Steenbeck**. The most common device for viewing and editing film in a cutting room.

**Storyboard**. A series of drawings showing the main scenes or set-ups in a film. Used most frequently in commercials.

**Synchroniser**. A device used in a film cutting room for running film and sprocketted tape in parallel to keep them synchronised.

**Theatrical release**. Showing of films or programmes in cinemas, television or on sale or rental of videocassettes, DVDs or similar.

**Trace and paint artists**. Artists who work on cells used in animation.

**Treatment**. A description in visual terms of the plot and characters of a film or television programme.

**Vision mixer**. Somebody in television who switches from one camera to another at the exact moment required and ordered by the director. The term also describes the equipment that does this action.

**Wrap**. The order to wrap up at the end of a day's shooting.

# Index